FAMILIES

THE FUTURE OF AMERICA

FAMILIES
THE FUTURE OF AMERICA

by

HAROLD M. VOTH, M.D.

Regnery Gateway
Chicago

Copyright © 1984 by Harold M. Voth, M.D. All rights reserved. Manufactured in the United States of America.

No part of this book may be produced in any manner whatsoever without written permission, except in the case of brief quotation embodied in critical articles and reviews.

Published by Regnery Gateway, Inc.
360 West Superior Street
Chicago, Illinois 60610-0890

Library of Congress Catalog
Card Number: 83-63266

ACKNOWLEDGEMENTS

I cannot name all of those wonderful people who have heard my speeches and lectures and whose encouragement led to the writing of this book. My gratitude is very great. I hope this book fulfills their expectations. I owe America a debt, for she gave me the freedom and the opportunity to develop my potential and make a contribution to life. She gave me a future; it is my hope that this book will help ensure hers.

I dedicate this book to my own family: to Patsy, my wife, to my sons, Eric and his wife Michelle (and to their little son), to Gregory and his wife Karen, and to Nicholas—and to those present and departed whose love and care helped make me what I am today.

TABLE OF CONTENTS

	Preface 9
Chapter I	A Changing America 13
Chapter II	The Family—The Source of Human and Social Vitality 19
Chapter III	The Disintegration of the Family 29
Chapter IV	The Signs of Social Sickness 39
Chapter V	Open *vs.* Committed Marriage 49
Chapter VI	The Women's Movement 61
Chapter VII	Unisexism 83
Chapter VIII	The "Normalization" of Homosexuality 89
Chapter IX	Pornography: A Barometer of the Nation's Sickness 99
Chapter X	The Drug Epidemic 119
Chapter XI	Parenting 147
Chapter XII	Can America Survive? A Call to Arms 153

PREFACE

It is usually taken for granted that stalwart Americans will always exist and that America will forever extend a protective wing over less powerful nations. But no generation is ever like the preceding one. New life replaces the old every moment. What are the new arrivals like? What values do they live by? Will they advance our way of life to new levels of excellence or will they adopt ways of life that lead to disintegration?

The basic fabric of our society is changing, and as it changes so do our people change. The trend is toward disintegration; a devitalizing process is at work, involving individual and social factors in a vicious and downhill cycle. A nation low in vitality and national will always loses out in one way or another to more vigorous nations. The interdigitation of personal and social factors is so firm that at present the future is by no means certain or clear. One can only hope that there will be enough people of strength, vision, and the capacity to take responsibility to intervene decisively before it is too late. The crucial question is whether or not the present trend in America is reversible.

The vitality of a nation is a reflection of the aggregate vitality of its people. In America we have been fortunate to have had the great energy of our people channeled by laws and customs which have permitted individuality to be expressed in such a way as to lead to social vitality and to excellence. People had the freedom to grow, innovate, create, and master great social challenges. We became the most powerful, efficient and generous nation of all time.

This book examines the American scene and explains why it is destroying itself and our children both literally and in spirit.

This is a tragic time in the history of our nation. Not too long ago parents could give their children a good start in life and be reasonably certain that the society into which they entered as children and young adults would not destroy them. This is no longer so. Even children from the most stable families are highly vulnerable to extremely destructive social forces. Illegitimate children, children from broken homes, and those from unstable families are virtually helpless with regard to the social revolution which will destroy them. Because of their weakness of personality they will be drawn into ways of living which not only destroy them, but they in turn will contribute to the destruction of our country by adopting these destructive ways of life.

In addition to social changes which are contributing to the destruction of people, young ones in particular, the family, from which all life springs, is crumbling. Families are breaking up at an alarming rate. Mothers are being forced by economic need to leave the home, or are by choice doing so. Babies and small children are not getting the kind of family life which prepares them for adult responsibilities.

Our nation will ultimately suffer. A nation has to be cared for like anything else. That is done by preserving its best traditions, customs, and social patterns and by socializing each new generation to embrace these values and advance them to new and higher levels of excellence. Strong, healthy people make strong societies. A nation filled with sick, devitalized people will eventually decline. This book will explain some of the reasons America is destroying itself.

Chapter I

A Changing America

It is an error to believe that America, the invincible, will always be. There is no Iron Law guaranteeing that generous and stalwart Americans will always exist. The American Dream is not forever safe. These ideas are illusions, born of self-deception. An internal process is at work in our country which poses a far greater danger to us than dwindling natural resources, the energy crisis, our huge national debt, or the trade deficit.

While it is true that technological advances, abundance of natural resources—in short, environmental and sociological factors—have a great deal to do with how far a society advances, personal factors or forces within the individual, that is, the vitality of a people, really make the difference. Social values, traditions, our constitutions, and laws channel individual vitality in ways that cause a people to develop into a great society or divert it in other directions. In America we have had the resources, the technological developments, the way of life, *and the individual vitality* which have made this the greatest nation of all time.

We are, however, all on a moving train. As we pass through this life, each individual supports certain values, traditions, and institutions and makes numerous contributions to society. Then suddenly death comes and our influence ends. New individuals take our place. But what will these new Americans be like? What values and patterns of living will they support? Will they advance our traditions and laws to new and higher levels of excellence, or will their ways of life lead to disintegration and decay? In my opinion, there is no question about the direction America is taking—we are deteriorating at an alarming rate. Not only is our way of life disintegrating but this very disintegration is destroying the spirits, that is, the vitality of our people. The young ones in particular are drawn into the mediocrity, decadence, and revolutionary ways that are altering our way of life.

America is caught in an exceedingly vicious spiral. Family life is failing and as a consequence a generation of children is being deprived of the kind of influences that can come only from the home, and of the good parenting which enables them to grow up to be strong, mature men and women. Put another way, strong-willed, energetic, creative, generous, emotionally healthy, and masterful people come from solid families. Such individuals easily embrace values, traditions, and laws which expect a great deal from them. They can do so because they possess great inner resources. Given the freedom from inner constraints or external barriers, it is in the nature of things for the human spirit to seek and find its highest level of achievement. Americans in the aggregate have demonstrated this principle.

The pattern of life in America is changing very

dramatically. The divorce rate is approaching 50% with second marriages failing at a rate close to 60%. Millions of young people are living together without taking the formal step of marriage. The illegitimacy rate is 20%. In large cities, the rate is much higher: 50% in Washington, D. C.; 33% in New York City, and 30% in Chicago. In Chicago alone that means 200,000 babies are born each year without a set of parents to rear them.

The simple truth is that the heterosexual bond, that is, the capacity for a man and a woman to remain lovingly committed to each other has become very fragile. This is an exceedingly ominous sign, for it is upon this bond that the fate of any society depends.

In addition to outright broken homes and situations which never were families, increasing numbers of marriages are severely strained, because of personality disturbances of the couple and social pressures. These strains and disturbances also have a profound effect on the developing child and eventually lead to personality disturbances of many different kinds in him.

Finally, the mass exodus of women from the home is having a damaging effect on young children. The work force is now one-half women. Forty-five per cent of these women have preschool children, and 50% or more have children of ages ranging up to adolescence. The absent mother has a disastrous effect on the development of the young, especially when the continuity of the mother-child relationship is broken during the first three years of life.[1]

It has been estimated that if these trends continue, within a few years nearly one-half of our young adults will have grown up in some arrangement other than the classical family for some portion of their development, that is, in a home where father was breadwinner and mother the homemaker. One study reported that today only 20% of our families are of the classical configuration, that is, the father as breadwinner and the mother at home with two or three small children. This is the kind of family that produced the solid people that made America the strongest nation of all time.

Emotionally sick parents or broken homes or part-time homes do not turn out high percentages of emotionally healthy boys and girls. Children from such homes grow up to be emotionally disturbed adults. Because of what is happening to the American family the number of emotionally disturbed people is increasing geometrically, that is, in ever-expanding numbers. Sick individuals eventually create a sick and weak society by changing the structure of their society and by weakening the national will. It is just that simple. I know of no possible way for America to retain its vitality, its preeminence among nations, with this trend in process. The family has produced people with the backbone, the spirit, the creativity, the productivity, and the strength to have made this nation what it became. Family life in America is crumbling like a sand castle in the way of a great wave of self-destruction.

In the following two chapters I will briefly outline the fundament developmental processes which lead to mature, responsible adulthood. This brief discussion provides a basis for understanding subsequent chapters which provide the evidence for the view that ours is a disintegrating society.

Chapter II

The Family—The Source Of Human And Social Vitality

Men and women and boys and girls must have a certain amount of vitality and freedom from crippling emotional illness to be able to get through life and not experience a sense of defeat when faced with life's challenges. There is nothing mysterious about emotional health and individual vitality, and we know very well what produces emotional illnesses which cripple and, at times, destroy people. I have worked as a psychiatrist for thirty years, and as a psychoanalyst for twenty, and the evidence that I have seen, as have many of my colleagues, is overwhelming as regard to what is required for babies and children to become healthy, mature men and women who can take hold of life, do something constructive with it, and embrace values, traditions, and institutions which advance the society. These strong people avoid those ways of life which destroy them as well as society itself.

The crucible from which all life springs is the family. The events within the family can make or break the individual, and collectively, the civilization. This fundamental unit is the building block, and has been the building block of all social organizations from the tribe, village, and on to the most highly developed societies and civilizations. Will Durant said the family can survive without the state, but without the family all is lost. Therefore, not only must the family survive, but its internal workings must function in ways that turn out strong men and women—not weak ones who eventually become casualties of one form or another or who may work actively against the best values and traditions of our country.

A newborn child contains great potential, but in order for that potential to be unlocked, evoked, developed, and expressed certain fundamental events must take place early in its life. When these events occur imperfectly or do not occur at all, the developing child will become a social liability in one form or another rather than an asset, or if he becomes an asset he may never achieve his full potential.

The underpinnings of personality are biologic underpinnings. None are more fundamental than the biologic imperatives which lead to the psychologic qualities of maleness and femaleness. There are, of course, an array of other potentialities. One of the most fundamental functions of parenting is to evoke, develop, and reinforce gender identity and then proceed to shepherd the developing child in such a way as to bring his psychological side into harmony with his biological side, and thereby develop a solid sense of maleness or femaleness.

Sexual identity is intimately woven into the overall fabric of personality. Human beings are not biologically bisexual, despite what the gay liberationists and some feminists would have us believe. The human spirit is greatly impaired when childhood development does not lead to fully developed masculinity or femininity. Fully masculine men and feminine women are by definition mature, and that term implies the ability to live out one's abilities. These include the capacity to mate, live in harmony with a member of the opposite sex, and carry out the responsibilities of parenthood. Mature people are competent and masterful; not only can they make families but they can take hold of life generally and advance it, and in particular they can replace themselves with healthy children who become healthy men and women. Mature individuals can, of course, elect to not have children and deploy all of their energies into their work. The fate of individual human development and of mankind depends on the durability of the heterosexual relationship, and the stability and integrity of the family.

The correct development of a child requires the commitment of mature parents who understand either consciously or intuitively that children do not grow up like Topsy. Good mothering from birth on provides the psychological core upon which all subsequent development takes place. *Mothering is probably the most important human function on earth.* This is a full-time, demanding task. It requires a high order of gentleness, commitment, steadiness, capacity to give, and many other qualities, too. A woman needs a good man by her side so she will not be distracted and depleted by too many other responsibilities. With his help, she will be able to provide rich humanness to her babies and children. Her needs must be met by the man. Above all, she must be made secure. A good man brings out the best in a woman, who can then do her best for the children. Similarly, a good woman brings out the best in a man, who can then do his best for his wife and children. Children bring out the best in their parents. All together they make a family, a place where people of great strength are shaped, who in turn make strong societies. Our nation was built by such people.

Strength of personality, individual vitality, competence, the capacity for mastery, the factors that make up a complete being, are not so mysterious. We know what kinds of experiences the developing child requires in order for him to develop these characteristics. These experiences are provided in the context of the classical family. At earlier times in our history social forces more readily permitted the expression of certain Laws of Nature which led to the formation of this classical family.

The heterosexual bond reflects the workings of one of Nature's most fundamental laws. The animal kingdom depends on it. Male and female are different and these qualities have biological underpinnings; that is, there are biologic laws that account for the difference between the sexes.[2] These differences attract each other and because of this attraction it is possible for the family to form as the young are born. There are laws that govern childhood development. When these are violated a great variety of personality disturbances result.

In order for the vast potentialities that lie locked in the biology of the newborn child to be realized, certain events must take place within the family. For these developmental processes to occur optimally, the child must have a feminine mother and a masculine father who are harmoniously committed to each other and to their children and family. Life was such in times past that the family could better flourish. Women were more feminine and more clearly recognized their highest and truest destiny, namely, the perpetuation of mankind. Men were more masculine; they made better husbands and fathers. More families remained intact and, as a consequence, percentage-wise, more children received good parenting.

The classical family which produces healthy boys and girls who become strong men and women is not a haphazard organization. Like all effective organizations it must follow operational principles. The principles which govern family life reflect the fundamental differences between male and female, and connect with certain developmental principles governing the growth of children. When these processes proceed smoothly children grow up relatively free of psychological conflicts and associated personality disturbances. Such adults grasp the challenges and opportunities of life and advance society to ever-higher levels of excellence. This is so because individual vitality seeks expression through the best existing values. Vital, masterful, and creative people create new values (laws, modes of conduct, etc.) which permit the maximal expression of their individuality for the good of society. This process accounts for the progress of civilization.

Numerous studies and observations have shown that the family structure which turns out the strongest men and women is that which has the man at the head of the family—not as a tyrant or dictator or someone who selfishly always gets his way, but one who is the ultimate source of strength, stability, and security for the entire family.[3] I believe Nature placed him there because of his greater physical strength, greater aggressiveness, greater dominance and his inner drive to establish territorial claims. He also possesses an enormously powerful protective instinct toward his mate and offspring. Men willingly lay down their lives for their families and they have done so for centuries. Mature men work very hard to provide for their families.

When the man responsibly attends to these biologic imperatives—and he will if unconscious conflicts within him do not stand in his way or if he is not prevented from doing so by external forces beyond his control—the woman can then function psychologically in accordance with those natural biological imperatives which define the female, the most obvious of which is the creation of new life. Above all, she will nurture her young and provide them with continuity of care. Her humanness is transmitted to the child by this continuous loving, gentle care and, as this process proceeds, the inner core of the child is formed.

All subsequent human development rests on this care. Later acquired skills are of little use without the inner core of security which is best provided by the natural mother, if she is mature. While the mothering and homemaking function is probably the most important of all human events, it is the least appreciated by society. I believe maternalism and homemaking are biological imperatives. Given the opportunity, with a good man by her side and in the absence of debilitating circumstances, a mature woman willingly fulfills her highest destiny, the one upon which mankind depends.

The simple truth is that there is no adequate substitute for a family. To be sure, children can grow up in other caretaking arrangements. But none equals a secure home and a mature mother and father, all the claims made by an assorted array of "experts" notwithstanding. Though father is the breadwinner and mother the homemaker, both should participate regularly in the events within the family. Both parents have a civilizing impact on the young. The mother touches them more directly when the children are small, while the father provides the authoritative stability for these processes. Ultimately daughters identify with their mothers and sons with their fathers. When this process has been completed, each sex is psychologically in harmony with its biology. The individual is not at cross purposes with himself. Then it remains for them to find a place in the environment where they can fully express what they have become. Obviously, ultimately finding a mate is part of this process. The remainder has to do with finding a social role within which the rest of the personality can be expressed. Such individuals inject great energy into the society in which they exist, and breathe life into society's best values.

Research studies and countless clinical reports provide scientific and clinical validation for what every student of the Bible knows. The Bible spells out these same principles for the organization of the family. In other words, the classical family works best and turns out the healthiest children. In my entire career I have never had a woman patient, no matter how militant a feminist or disturbed, fail to spontaneously divulge her secret wish for a strong man in her life—father when she was a child and husband as an adult woman, even though on the surface she may claim the opposite.

A woman who can live in harmony with a strong man will herself be a strong woman. These two will not clash or compete with each other. Rather they will divide up responsibilities, and live and work in harmony. I did not create or manufacture these patterns; I am merely reporting them. It is simply a fact that a family with a weak man suffers and children do not turn out as well.

When the personalities of parents are crippled by psychological conflicts, in particular those which impair a clear sense of maleness or femaleness, or when children are deprived of the continuous commitment of mothers and fathers (the mother in particular) during the first few years of life, developmental disturbances occur in children of varying degrees of severity, depending on the time and duration of parental absence or the degree of severity of the personality disturbances in the parents. The developmental disturbances in the children may show up in childhood, or they may go underground only to surface years later when life begins to make its demands on them, especially when they attempt to make families of their own.

Those pioneers who developed America possessed great inner strength. They came from strong families. There was no ambiguity about male or female. Their will prevailed because they had received generously from their mothers and fathers. Fathers were men of strength, direction, and authority. Family ties were close and solid. America became the greatest, strongest, and most generous nation of all time.

Books, and scientific and clinical articles exist in great abundance which describe in detail the nature of the developmental process which leads to mature, emotionally healthy adults. It is not my intent to describe these processes in this book; I have done that elsewhere—see the comparison piece to this book.[4]

Chapter III

The Disintegration of the Family

Industrialization slowly unraveled the close and continuous tapestry of family life. Inexorably fathers were seen less and less; mothers had to take over more of the husbands' responsibilities and as a consequence they had less time and energy to discharge the mothering function. Cities grew, commuting distances increased, and families became uprooted. Then came wars—World War I, World War II, and Korea. Fathers were killed, millions were taken away for long periods of time, and others came back a shell of what they once were. More and more children were denied a good family life because of these losses or absences. Not only were fathers away, but mothers had to devote time and energy to tasks other than the rearing of children and homemaking. The children of these families suffered the consequences. They in turn could not do well as parents when their turn came, and on and on through each successive generation.

Economic pressures also did enormous damage to families. Millions were and are disrupted by the mothers being forced to work. Even more babies and children were and are deprived of good parenting. The number of babies and children who are now deprived of good family life is staggering! When a child is denied good parenting, he develops personality disturbances of one kind or another, he passes these psychological difficulties on to his children, and ultimately society loses its vitality as the number of disturbed people increases with each generation.

The most common circumstances which impair childhood development include maternal absence or separations from the infant and child, the absent father, personality disturbances of the parents, strained relationship between the parents and, of course, the outright broken home. The circumstance which renders the child most vulnerable to disturbed psychological development is the single parent home where that parent is a woman who for reasons of her own cannot live with a man in harmony. Very domineering and aggressive women and weak, passive, and irresponsible men are equally damaging to the developing child.

The most common consequence of the psychological disturbances which are the result of faulty childhood development is the diminished ability to form a durable heterosexual bond and within that bonding to carry out the parenting function. This incapacity, which vast and ever-increasing numbers of Americans have, is reflected in the high illegitimacy rate, the high divorce rate, and in the large number of people who live together without the formal bond of marriage. I also believe the exodus of the woman out of the home when children are still young (in the absence of pressing economic need) also reflects the incapacity to carry out the parenting function. This lack, or deficit, is just as prevalent in the man, but it is less obvious because of his traditional role as breadwinner. The truth of the matter is that increasing numbers of men fail as adequate husbands and fathers just as women are failing in their role as wives and mothers.

When little girls and little boys do not receive optimal parenting as I earlier described it, the most common consequence is fearfulness about becoming feminine and masculine and living out that identity in an appropriate social role. As a consequence of their fears and other psychological disturbances, females tend to become overcontrolling, often domineering, frequently hostile toward men, and competitive with them. These traits provide a certain degree of self-protection but clash with the basic biologic imperatives of the woman. Men tend to become weak, passive, even effeminate, and usually somewhat irresponsible. Some men can live out their natural aggressiveness and dominance at work but are fearful in relation to the women in their lives. These traits in men, similarly, have a self-defensive function.

The natural condition between male and female throughout the animal kingdom is harmony. Male and female clash or do open battle only at the human level. This is so because of psychological conflicts within the man and woman which prevent them from living out the marvelous harmony Nature provides for. Those damaging psychological conflicts are created during childhood development. The more disturbed or broken the family life of the child, the greater and more severe will his psychological conflicts or disturbance become.

I think there is little question that the social revolution and the progressive decline of our society that has beset this nation is the outgrowth of these psychological changes in millions of men and women. What we are seeing on a national level is a trend toward unisexism and, even worse, outright role reversal. There is enormous tension between the sexes. On balance the feminists are winning and because they are, men are losing, the family is losing out, society is losing, and ultimately so are women.

Furthermore, virtually every form of psychopathology or disturbance in human behavior is increasing. There is nothing surprising about this at all. The psychological conflicts which form during the child's developmental years are in virtually all of the psychological disturbances known to afflict mankind.

When sufficient numbers of sick people exist, they leave their imprint on the structure of society. This happens because these vast numbers of people form alliances or organizations; leaders emerge from their ranks, and they set about to change society so as to accommodate them.

When the psychopathology is grossly deviant in its form, society continues to label the behavior as illness. For instance, it will probably never happen that child abuse will some day be viewed as a form of normal behavior. On the other hand, homosexuality which, until a few years ago, was generally viewed as a form of psychological illness, is now being viewed by many, including some professionals, as a normal variant of sexuality. Committed marriage once was the only norm; now the open marriage and variations thereof are viewed as normal. Classically, women have been considered best equipped psychologically to be homemakers; now the "househusband" is part of the social scene. A few years ago it would have been unthinkable to have women drill sergeants for young male recruits, and on and on.

As the number of maladjusted people increases, they alter the environment through political action so as to accommodate their psychopathology. It is always easier to change the environment so as to accommodate what you are rather than to have to change (for the better, that is, become more mature) in order to meet the expectations (for mature behavior) of the environment. By way of analogy, if a child cannot function well enough in school to make an A, or simply to pass, then lower the expectations and he will pass. The only problem is that the level of excellence falls. Excellence is disappearing in our land.

A separate chapter of this book is devoted to the feminist movement. However, at this point, reference to that movement provides the most dramatic example of how the environment is being altered as a consequence of the psychological conflicts of millions of women. I wish to be clearly understood in that I favor many of the changes this movement has brought about, but there is a clear and powerful element of psychopathology in it too. This psychopathology derives directly from the disturbed childhood development millions of women experienced as a consequence of the severe social assaults the family has suffered over the past seventy-five years or so. Men have undergone this disturbed development too, but men have not needed a movement; they have had an easy escape from parenting and husbandly responsibilities simply because they go to work every day. Millions of women are "liberating" themselves from homemaking and family responsibilities because their (unconscious) psychological conflicts make the mothering and homemaking functions unbearable to them.

Again, while the feminist movement proceeded to some extent from a legitimate base, in that it strove to correct genuine inequities and also to make some of the newer aspects of our modern society available to women, I believe that a powerful force within that movement derives from psychological disturbances within the deeper regions of the minds of many of the militant leaders. All one has to do is look at their aggressive, often brassy, and even masculinized ways, and the disturbances within many of them is quickly obvious. Show me a militant feminist and I wager I can almost always reveal the psychopathology within her (if she will cooperate) that motivates her and I will also point out the disturbances in her parents and her childhood experiences which created these emotional problems.

For instance, one feminist leader is quoted as having said, when discussing the vocational and professional achievements of women, "We are becoming the men we wanted to marry." This remark beautifully captures what I believe is an underlying motivation of many feminists. Because so many women cannot make family life successful or satisfying, they must alter the environment so as to accommodate what they are trying to become. Many of these women do not just want equal opportunity with men; they want superiority over them. They want to dominate the male. This trend is reflected by a new organization in New York, the avowed purpose of which is to convert America from a patriarchy to a matriarchy. They are recruiting a very large following. The influence of such women through various organizations, particularly the communications media, is enormous—much greater than most people recognize. And what are the men doing? They are backing down like frightened little boys in the face of any angry, domineering mother upon whose goodwill they depend. The militant feminists are having their way in virtually every aspect of American life—in the Congress, in the courts, in industry, in schools, in television and radio programming, in communications of all kinds, and in the family. These patterns are absolutely what is to be expected in view of what has happened to family life over the past seventy-five years or so. The effects on our society are enormous. Not only is this movement directly destructive to the family, it breeds war between the sexes, and often places women in positions where they should not be, such as military combat.

These millions of people, men and women alike, who are turning their backs on the family—the one they would like to create but cannot, or the one they have created—are literally driven away from their home and parenting responsibilities by forces within themselves. They heed Nature's call on a biological level in one way or another, but they cannot follow through psychologically for a sustained period sufficiently prolonged so as to be able to properly launch the new life they create, and thereby bring forth a new generation of emotionally healthy children. The trend is in a negative direction; unless it is reversed, this nation is doomed. Bear in mind only seventeen generations have passed over this land since Columbus discovered America. It will only take a few generations to fill the nation with such glut of emotionally disturbed, weakened people that we will tear ourselves apart or become vulnerable to a stronger outside force.

I discussed the part good family life plays in the life of the developing children so that they are able to grow up to be strong, competent, masterful men and women. Conversely, severe strain within the home, personality disturbances in parents, and the outright broken home have damaging effects on the developing child. Millions of Americans contain within them forces which, under certain circumstances, will make them seriously ill. Many already are emotionally ill. When widely enough spread, certain forms of emotional illness eventually change society. Sick people and sick societies have a very powerful feedback effect on individuals, especially the younger ones entering the social scene. Today sick people are changing the social scene. I believe it is having an enormously destructive feedback effect on our young people. In subsequent chapters I will discuss some of the more obvious ways society is harming and destroying our young.

Chapter IV
The Signs of Social Sickness

The breakdown of family life, the part-time families, the single-parent families, and the sick families create the psychological disturbances in the developing child which sooner or later will emerge as a behavioral disturbance or a frank psychiatric illness. It is inevitable that the prevalence of classical psychopathology is increasing. The forms of these disturbances are highly varied. What follows are some examples of the obvious sickness in millions of our fellow Americans. Some of these illnesses like homosexuality, drug usage, pornography, etc. will be discussed in greater detail in special chapters. These chapters were written in order to provide a deeper view of the gravity of the problems facing us.

Alcoholism and drug use are virtually at an epidemic level. While it is true that drugs and alcohol have direct habituating and addictive effects, the primary reason people ingest chemicals is to calm their anxiety or remove depression. It is no mystery why millions of our youth are using drugs. They are psychologically unready to master the challenges of life. Instead of looking to the future with anticipation and joy, they are fearful of experiencing a sense of defeat. They turn to chemicals to calm or energize them-

40   *Families*

selves. The annual eighty-billion-dollar street drug business in our country is a shocking and alarming barometer of the psychological condition of millions of our fellow Americans. Without access to marijuana, cocaine, heroin, and other drugs, millions of Americans, most of whom are youthful, would have to face reality and/or ask for help rather than take the easier, retrogressive, escapist route. Drug pushers are criminals of the worst kind; they profit from human weakness and illness and, along with the sick users, are seriously damaging our society. Study after study reveals serious family disturbances in the drug user—not in all, to be sure, but in most of them.[5] Even healthy people can get hooked on drugs; this fact shows what powerful and destructive substances drugs are. The damage to the individuals who use drugs and the damage they in turn do to society through lowered efficiency is enormous.

When drugs fail, suicide is the final step in the admission of defeat. Suicide is now the second or third most common cause of death of the young. On the threshold of life many of our young people are ending their lives. This phenomenon is not surprising; in fact, it is predictable in view of the disintegration of the family. These desperate young people lack the inner resources to face life, and master it.

Child abuse and spouse abuse have become a national disgrace. The American family has recently been defined as one of the most violent places on earth. Physical and sexual assaults have reached a shocking level. These phenomena are not mysterious. The abuser was abused and neglected as a child. As an adult he lacks the patience required of parents. The sexual molester failed to mature psychosexually. The root causes stand out in sharp relief when a retrospective study is made of these violent and abusive individuals. This trend can be expected to increase.

School violence is so bad, what with rape and assault on teachers, that a new syndrome—combat neurosis for school teachers—has been proposed. Droves of our best teachers are resigning because of the chaos in the classroom. These violent children are enraged, primarily because of the deprivations within the context of their family life, and only secondarily because of the social conditions in which they live. Furthermore, lacking an inner authority, they assault (70,000 times in one year) and rape, and even murder the most benevolent external authority—the school teacher.

The flourishing pornography business provides one of the most ominous barometers of the state of emotional health of millions of Americans. Emotional health is achieved through proper childhood development in a healthy family. Conversely, emotional disturbances of which psychosexual disorders are a major component, are a product of disturbed home life. X-rated movies and pornography rarely depict mature sexuality. Pornography depicts the perversions and the debasement of women, and this business flourishes simply because of its wide and increasing appeal to millions of Americans.

Homosexuality is not biologically caused. The causes are to be found in childhood development within the context of disturbed family life. Typically the father is weak or absent and the mother is overly possessive, domineering, or insecure. Wars always cause a crop of homosexuals because fathers are away. The condition is increasing in prevalence and will continue to do so. Rampant homosexuality is one of the signs of societies in crisis or in a state of collapse. The gay movement is an extremely ominous sign because of the significance of the phenomenon. Equally ominous is the remarkable success the gays are having in convincing segments of our society that theirs is a normal condition. Fortunately, clear-thinking and healthy people have not yielded to this propaganda. Even so, homosexual values are finding their way into schools, including medical schools, books, even into the courts (as when a homosexual was appointed as a Superior Court Judge), and into the very fabric of our culture, alongside the unisex propaganda that boys and girls are essentially the same.

There exists no clearer example of how individual psychopathology leads to social pathology. A key element in the gay banner is the view that bisexuality is the norm, not heterosexuality. While you and I are immune to this poisonous propaganda, the vulnerable young are not. It is appalling to see so many school teachers subscribe to these views. The laws of Nature are strong, but man has the capacity to override them, and when he does he destroys himself. The so-called "normalization" of homosexuality and the obliteration of the differences between the sexes

The Signs of Social Sickness 43

is the major element in the destructive processes now underway.

Several observers have stated that the trend in the nation is for individuals to become more selfish, egoistic, and narcissistic. Generosity, altruism, and selflessness result from high parental input of love, care, and devotion to the young. The young can then in turn be giving and generous as adults.

No better indicator exists of the deterioration of standards governing sexuality than the illegitimacy rate. One-half of the nation's annual product of 13.5 million babies who will be born to mothers between 18 and 24 years old will be illegitimate. Unmarried black women of that same age range will bear two-thirds of all the babies, that is to say, 78% of the black babies of that 13.5 million will not have a father. I believe the nation's overall rate of illegitimacy is around 20%. Thirty percent of the births in Chicago (200,000) each year are illegitimate, 33% in New York City, and 50% in Washington, D. C. It is estimated that 45% of the babies born in 1976 will be living with a single parent before they are 18 years old. These births go on year after year after year. In twenty years one-half of the young Americans will not have grown up in a solid family.

It is no surprise that the Presidential Commission on Mental Health estimates that 8 million American children need immediate help for psychiatric disorders. I have read estimates which reach 30 million.[6] I believe the latter figure. In view of the disintegration of the durability of the male-female bond, the collapse of so many families, and the inability to make a complete bond by those who attempt it, that figure is or surely will be merely an indication of what is to come.

As developmental disturbances occur in increasing numbers of people, their performance in society—that is to say, their competence, masterfulness, productiveness, and quest for excellence—suffers. Psychologically disturbed people simply do not have the inner resources to work hard, to find joy in ever-improving their performances, to create, to innovate, and so on. Instead, they drift toward mediocrity or failure. Millions of our people in almost all walks of life reflect these changes.

Students at all levels generally do not perform as they once did; there are exceptions, of course. A recent survey of university professors revealed a longing in them for the old days when students strained themselves in their quest for excellence. In the large cities children are several grades behind those in the smaller communities. Inevitably, standards are lowered. Standardized test scores continue their decline.

Even in the face of modern medicine, venereal disease is again at the epidemic level, with new types added to gonorrhea and syphilis. The herpes virus is now classed as a venereal disease and homosexuals are transmitting hepatitis (viral infection of the liver) through their practice of anal intercourse. The rise of venereal disease is an indicator of the unrestrained sexual patterns which are sweeping across the nation. As in ancient Rome, it is difficult to find a virgin (of either sex) any more.

The most alarming sign of social decay is the reappraisal of the meaning of incest and what society's response should be to it. In Sweden an attempt was made to decriminalize incest. In the United States a certain social worker is leading a "movement" to re-examine the phenomenon. He claims that all incest may not be bad, and that the child is not necessarily harmed by parent-child sexual relations.[7]

The two most fundamental taboos of civilization are cannibalism and incest. The reasons should be obvious to every thinking person. The prohibition of sexual relations within families is a key element in personality development and the civilizing process. The very fact that serious consideration is being given to adopting a permissive attitude toward incest is unquestionably the most serious sign of all with regard to the decay of our society.

The abolition of the incest taboo would be the endpoint of the current trend in society toward ever greater direct gratification of the instinctual side of life. Some gratification is, of course, necessary, but much of our instinct and energy forms the basis for the creative process and cultural development. Cultural growth is lagging, the quest for excellence is disappearing—predictably—as the instincts and the senses are ever more directly gratified through drugs, freewheeling sexual styles, pornography and near-pornographic movies, plays and publications, homosexuality, child prostitution, an overall decline in morality, and now, possibly, God forbid, incest itself.

Viewing any of these developments in isolation

fails to reveal the big picture. The tendency is to brush off swinging sexual styles as a passing fad, or the "normalization" of homosexuality as a transient event which will in time pass away, or pornography as harmless if you do not let your children get hooked, or the re-evaluation of incest as the workings of the misguided mind of a kook, etc. By lumping all these moral developments together, by backing off and viewing them from a distance, *and* by looking into the psychopathology in the personalities of those who embrace the developments, in particular their champions, *then* you begin to really see and understand the extent of our disintegration. Some brush all this aside and claim that the next generation will clear all this up, assuming, with this claim, that wisdom and emotional health automatically appear with every new generation. They do not.

In summary, whether the changes reflect an increase in the typical forms of psychopathology, the increased use of chemicals, the divorce rate, the illegitimacy rate, the violence we do to each other (both in the home and in society), the changes in sexual mores, changes in lifestyle, changes in productivity and standards (excellence), and changes in the American character itself (toward unisexism), there can be no doubt that all signs point to deterioration, decay, and decline. The rest of the world knows it too. Other nations are taking liberties with us which not too many years ago they could never have dreamed of doing. Our weakness is reflected in our low productivity, our weakened military, and irresolute national leadership. One day the challenge will face us; our very survival as a nation will be at stake. I repeat, collapsing family life leads to sick children who become sick adults who create a sick nation. Strong nations always dominate weak ones. It is a law of Nature. Strength always dominates over weakness.

Chapter V
Open vs. Committed Marriage

Earlier I said the solid monogamous family unit is the source of maturity and strength. This arrangement provides stability and security for children *and* the impact of a man and a woman into their developing personalities. Mothering and fathering in the psychological sense is just as important as the biological act of creating a new life. Children will undergo physiological changes, and outwardly they will appear to grow up in almost any set of circumstances. However, for children to become strong men and women who are clear about their gender and who can master life, a solid family unit is required for the human spirit to achieve maximum potential.

In mature people the heterosexual bond can be very strong and will be if a love relationship develops. Heterosexual bonding, unlike male-to-male bonding, is very private and possessive. Male-to-male bonding is seen at its best in the Armed Forces when men band together in order to achieve a common goal. In these circumstances men will give their lives to protect others in pursuit of their common goal. Male-male bonding does not refer to homosexual relationships. Male-male bonding can involve two males or many; it does not depend on the sexual element. Male-female bonding, on the other hand, does involve sexuality and while polygamy has existed, the overwhelming pattern is monogamous.

What then shall be made of "marital" styles, such as open marriage, swinging, living-together arrangements which are not formalized, and plain infidelity? Evidence abounds to support the view that an emotionally mature man and women will find monogamy fully satisfying. It has been conclusively shown that those who do not adhere to this pattern are usually driven by emotional conflicts away from their marital commitment and into other kinds of relationships. Young people who are on the threshold of life and marriage need to fully understand this. Many who are emotionally disturbed will sooner or later find their marriage less than adequately satisfying and it may become deeply strained. It is an illusion to believe that extramarital affairs or a swinging style or agreeing upon the so-called "open marriage" arrangement will solve their problems. Such methods will only make matters worse, and will hasten the total destruction of the marriage.

I never cease to be astounded by how blindly and frequently people follow some self-appointed "expert's" advice on how to live life. A recent example is the book called *The Open Marriage*.[8] It is my understanding that at least two million copies of this book have been sold. Recently one of the authors (a married couple whose field is sociology) admitted that every couple they knew who followed the guidelines which are spelled out in their book, has ended up divorcing.

I am very glad I do not have all those divorces on my conscience!

When the man or woman or both have a sexual relationship with someone other than their spouse, or when one or both members of a marriage become excessively involved with others and exclude the spouse, the bond weakens and eventually breaks. The possessive element in male-female bonding simply cannot, for very long, withstand the assault of infidelity. Sooner or later the marriage will break up. Sometimes the marriage will last officially, but the true marriage will have disappeared.

I believe those individuals who espouse these various "marital" styles are doing so because of their own emotional conflicts. I know this to be so in many instances through my professional work. These "marital" styles reflect the inability to make a total and satisfying commitment to a member of the opposite sex. That inability is due to emotional conflicts and those are the product of the individual's personality development. Volumes have been written on this subject.

Childhood conflicts having to do with love and sex, guilt co-operation, domination, submission, gender identity, intimacy, etc. which live on in the unconscious region of the mind are the primary reasons men and women cannot succeed in monogamous marriage even though they may love each other very much. The process of committing oneself to a member of the opposite sex triggers those unconscious conflicts. The emotionally strained person must then find a way to create distance from the conflict triggering factor (the spouse) and, of course, the best ways to do that are to start a fight, be unfaithful, or withdraw.

All of these strategies lead to emotional distance. Some simply quietly withdraw from the spouse. Others grow dissatisfied on one pretext or another spontaneously, or after having provoked the spouse who quite naturally withdraws, and they seek gratification outside marriage. This is usually done after having generated an ample supply of rationalization for the infidelity. While sometimes true incompatibility does exist between marital couples, the more common basis for the failure of the marriage are those residues of childhood experiences which exist in the form of emotional conflicts in the unconscious region of the mind.

What we are seeing in society today is a progressive crumbling of the building blocks of society. I am referring to broken marriages, now occurring at the 50% rate. Quite naturally those who cannot succeed in monogamous marriage create other ways for finding at least partial gratification for their human needs. Though they cannot live in marriage, they still hunger for human closeness, sexual outlets, the wish to be parents, and so on. They try swinging, open marriages, communes, being together without marriage, and the like. These ways of living reflect failure and should never be held up to the young as a suitable way to live life.

If I were a young man and found a young woman who was willing to live with me without the formal commitment of marriage, I would drop her as a prospective wife. Her behavior would be saying she lacked the strength of character, the maturity, the freedom from unconscious conflicts to be able to hold out for higher status and greater reward, namely, a full-fledged marriage.

Statistics show that the divorce rate is higher in couples who have lived together before marriage than in those who court each other and then marry. Living together does not reflect freedom from psychological and sexual conflicts—just the opposite in most instances. Living together implies difficulty with loving and sexual commitment. This deficit is ultimately reflected in the higher divorce rate. That is to say, when the couple who have been living together finally marry in the formal sense, something happens to upset an equilibrium. The greater degree of committment triggers unconscious conflicts that had lain relatively dormant. Having been triggered, they produce internal discomfort (anxiety, guilt, etc.). "Incompatibility" then begins to appear between the couple, creating distance between them. This distance in turn reduces the conflict each is having on the other, and their own unconscious conflicts sink into the deeper regions of the mind. Less inner discomfort is felt by both parties, even though they may experience some distress about the distance between them.

If my spouse agreed to a swinging arrangement, or demanded an open marriage, I would conclude she no longer loved me (our bond had dissolved), or that she was being impinged upon by her unconscious conflicts. I would know for certain that our marriage was probably doomed unless her psychiatric disturbance was successfully treated and/or her love could be rekindled.

Beware of the proponents of these alternate marital styles. An example of how the personality and personal conflicts (emotional disturbances) of the proponent is probably the true basis for their theory can be found in Margaret Mead. This lady, who was so preoccupied with what is male and female, once said (I heard her) monogamy was not the answer for mankind. Clearly not in her view, for she was married and divorced three times. The so-called "masculinity complex" stood out in her like a sore thumb. She believed she had inherited her father's brain. I think she identified with her father instead of her mother, and the resultant psychological conflicts made it impossible for her to live in harmony with a man. Many thousands of people have been influenced by this woman.

The most glaring expression of her emotional conflicts was her public endorsement of a lesbian "marriage" and the recommendation that these women be given custody of five children.

Doctor Mead is only one example of how professional people, and even scientists, can be influenced by forces within the unconscious region of the mind. Virtually every professional in the field of psychiatry, psychoanalysis, and psychology that I have known has shown some evidence of this. The mental health fields attract people with emotional disturbances, and while some of these work out their problems, many do not. Psychoanalysts must undergo a personal analysis in addition to their training before they can be certified as analysts. This is a fine requirement, but even this "safety factor" by no means is proof that the values analysts live by and practice are free from unconscious disturbances.

This issue is worth much more than a paragraph or two because many who cannot make formal marriage succeed eventually seek professional assistance. Be *very careful* whom you select as a helper. If they espouse values which deviate too far from the classical guidelines for marriage, you will be wise to drop them.

Unfortunately some of the most severe emotional disturbances surface in the context of marriage. Sometimes simple counselling is all that is required; often thorough treatment is needed. While these remarks are helpful to individuals, the great problem is the 50% divorce rate. Some of these people will eventually mature and their subsequent marriages will succeed. The divorce rate can only drop if a huge number of emotionally healthy children are again launched into adulthood. Only then can marriage flourish once again.

Those who think they are being sophisticated by adopting open marriage arrangements are fooling themselves. They are simply trying to mask their inability to become or remain (if they once were) fully committed to their spouse. The wealthier classes and the intellectuals more often tend to go for these non-committed arrangements. They are troubled by unconscious conflicts, but do not know it. By moving away from each other they are able to stay married and at the same time gratify various needs in their relationship with others. A high price is paid for these arrangements. Missing is that marvelous sense of intimacy which characterizes a mature relationship. Instead, these couples have to settle for fragmented lives and miss out on the intensity and closeness that comes from a total commitment to spouse and children.

In my other book I spelled out in more detail why men and women cannot experience intimacy in marriage.[9]

I suggest you read that book, particularly the chapter on the normal family, childhood development, and the chapter on why people become ill and fail to succeed in life, including in marriage, and the chapter on self-help.

My best advice to newlyweds and even those who have been married for longer periods is to *not* give up if strife and/or dissatisfactions enter your marriage. Hold steady and work very hard to overcome your differences. You will both mature if you do, and as more mature people, you will be much better parents. It is always more difficult to mature than to give up and slide back into sick or immature ways of behavior. But the rewards for maturing are enormous. The gratifications associated with giving in to your immaturies are usually immediate, but in the long run you will pay a very high price. You will usually be doomed to repeating your old patterns with another mate, and to have your marriage fail again; nearly two-thirds of second marriages do. The loneliness of life can be very severe when your family breaks up, especially as you enter the middle and final years. Those who think they are in such a fine bed of roses after renouncing family life are in for a rude shock as they get older, particularly men and women who have had children.

To sum up: Because family life has been so badly damaged over the past several generations, many millions of children have been denied the best kind of mothering and fathering and family life. As a consequence, our society is filled with millions of adults who cannot make family life succeed; hence, the high divorce rate, the high illegitimacy rate, the large number of people who live together in various kinds of arrangements short of marriage and so on. Quite naturally, these individuals wish to legitimize or "normalize" their life styles. That is, they are altering the rules of the game—the values of society—to suit their personal inadequacies. It is always easier to bring standards down to your level rather than have to rise up to higher standards. It is very easy to find "professional" help which will help you lower your standards, and dupe you into believing you have been successfully treated. A large enough number of people can change standards and social norms according to their wishes. I see these alternatives to committed, faithful monogamy as expressions of individual psychopathology. Large numbers of emotionally disturbed people lead to a sick society. Ultimately society becomes weakened. Remember, a solid male-female bond is the foundation for the family; solid, strong families are the base for the creation of strong societies.

These remarks add up to mean that if you cannot find happiness in a regular, old-fashioned marriage something is wrong. Fix that which is wrong and save your marriage if you possibly can. Your happiness, the proper emotional development of your children, and ultimately the future of America depend upon you. If you are having trouble, read the companion piece to this book. I believe you will find helpful guidelines there.[10]

A final word about the maturational process should cause you to conclude reading this chapter with more courage and a greater sense of hope if you are finding marriage difficult or threatening. Remember, it is in the nature of things for maturation to occur. Plant a seed and it grows into a tree. We are all destined toward a final form. However, in order for that growth to occur properly we must interact properly with the environment. Within the environment there are factors which inhibit growth and push us backwards toward earlier immaturity and there are factors which stimulate growth and maturation. Therefore, we have two kinds of allies which help us mature. These are internal natural pressures toward maturity, and external factors which stimulate growth. The latter refer largely to the responsibilities of life. In other words, if you will shoulder life's responsibilities, you will mature unless you are so badly burdened by emotional conflicts (latent illness) that you become ill in the attempt.

Therefore, stick by your marital commitments, and your parental responsibilities, *and* give yourself time to change; that is, to mature. Remember it takes time for dough to rise and be ready for the final baking. Similarly, people generally do not mature overnight. No environmental factor has a greater maturational impact on the individual than a child, *if* the parents are committed to it. *Be* a mother and a father, and you will be setting yourself up for the greatest possible emotional growth; you will be providing invaluable impact for your child and society will ultimately benefit enormously. Do not turn tail and run during periods of stress and strain.

Chapter VI

The Women's Movement

The Women's Liberation movement is a complex development in modern society. There are many motivations within it; some are highly constructive and some are highly destructive. People tend to lose their objectivity when discussing the movement and that, of course, is unfortunate. At issue is how individuals fulfill themselves, make meaningful and constructive contributions to society, *and* create new lives which will grow up to be emotionally healthy men and women who can, in turn, perpetuate life.

In the past, in large part, the male was breadwinner and the female did the homemaking. In those times, the father participated in family life. The division of responsibilities were rather clear. On the farm, families worked together, but even there women tended the house, the chickens, separated cream from milk, canned, etc., while the men did the heavier work in the fields.

There can be no question that modern labor-saving devices have freed the time of women, and accordingly, they have turned to the work force and to the institutions of higher learning to find additional purpose for their lives. Since society outside the home was filled largely by men, and since men were the breadwinners, society rewarded the male who, in turn, rewarded (provided for) his family. Now society rewards many more women directly as a consequence of their having entered the work force.

There is no question that women have been discriminated against. They have had no spokesman or organization to look after their interests. In the free market it is inevitable that they would be exploited, that is, the effort would be made to get as much out of them for as little as possible. But this process is not unique to women. Men have exploited other men (and boys) for centuries. Getting as much for as little as possible is the name of the game. Social processes are at work which are correcting these inequities, injustices, and prejudices against women and much progress has been made. To this end the Women's Liberation movement has had a very constructive effect on our way of life. Many inequities remain, however, for *both* men and women; it will be a long time before the best possible reward system is worked out for what the individual contributes to society.

Recently some attention has turned to "the worth" of the homemaker. This individual has truly been lost in the massive reordering of society. Obviously, there is no standard worth. Some homemakers are magnificent women. Some have also functioned as teachers, skillful advisors, politicians, hostesses, etc., etc. Others were little more than shrews who made everyone miserable and thoroughly damaged the psychological development of their children. In short, women, their social roles and the rewards that are due them are getting a great deal of attention these days.

In addition to the time-freeing effect modernization has had for women, the ravages of inflation have forced many women into the work force who otherwise would have preferred to stay at home. Many of these women are untrained, and, therefore, by necessity must accept lower-paying positions, a fact which appears discriminatory when their income and positions are fed into the statistics, but in reality is not. Their finest skills are expressed in the home, but they are forced out into the work force by economic need. *That* is discriminatory.

One of the battle cries of the feminists is this very point—if women did not spend so much time making families, they would not lose out in the work force; they would not be handicapped by having been out of the running. They see a grave injustice in this fact. They fail to see that the homemaker has a career and that when she enters the work force she is building a second one. Their rebuttal is that had they not dropped out of their professional work, or left their jobs to make a family, they could be much further along in the hierarchy. That is undoubtedly true in many instances. However, none seem to pause and ask the central question: Would they trade their lovely, healthy children and the rich life they created for everyone by making a home for higher rank in their profession or a higher position in the company? Do they think men have never turned down promotions or advancement in order not to have to uproot their families?

One solution of the women's liberationists' (at least of some of them) is to divide up child care equally. Soon after the birth of the child, they propose that the woman and man should share equally in the child's care. By each working half-time at their jobs, the infant and child would receive equal amounts of parenting from both mother and father. By this method the woman would not lose out in the work force.

It is quite true that both parents are necessary for the best possible psychological development for the child. However, the importance of mothering and fathering vary at different stages of the child's development. In the beginning, the mother's care, devotion and the relative constancy of her presence is paramount. No one can adequately take the place of the biologic and mature mother to whom the infant becomes bonded. A father's personality is different from the mother's, and his impact on the child is different. These basic truths exist whether certain factions of society like to admit it or not.

Some parents believe the infant or small baby can be turned over to a caretaker or day-care center so they can return to their work. They cite studies which purport to show that children develop just as well in these situations, as those who are reared by full-time parents. Measuring human qualities is very difficult, particularly the capacity to love, to be committed to people and to work, to be masterful and so on. Furthermore, the kinds of emotional disturbances which result from poor child care frequently do not surface until adulthood when the responsibility of life must be shouldered, especially those associated with a loving and committed relationship to the opposite sex and the making of a family. The most solid and healthy families are created by those who grew up in such families.

These few paragraphs have introduced the destructive aspects of the Women's Liberation movement. In their rush to enter the labor force they are literally throwing the baby out with the bath. They are losing sight of the absolutely essential place the family has for mankind. It appears as if they do not believe the family is important, or if it has some importance, it ranks low in the scale. How can this be? The question to be addressed is why have women turned away from the home in such large numbers. Why are so many women becoming hostile toward men, so competitive with them, and so envious of the social role men have traditionally filled? Why are men so meekly standing aside? Bear in mind that men are turning away from marital and family responsibilities too, but they are less visible because they do not have a "Men's Liberation Movement" organization to represent them.

The exodus from the family is easily understandable. One need only reflect on the source or the capacity to bond with the opposite sex, to be a parent, and to find great fulfillment in that experience. When one is not prepared for these high privileges, one must do something else with his life. No one can live in a vacuum, everyone must connect with the environment somewhere.

I have several times referred to changes in the

American character. I will now go into this in somewhat greater detail and thereby present a clearer picture of what is happening to us and the implication of these changes for future families and for our society.

The evolutionary trend within the animal kingdom, it must be clearly understood, is toward sexual differentiation and sexual dimorphism. At the level of man, male and female are clearly distinguishable, in contrast to lower forms of animal life where sexual differences are less extreme. Psychologically, male and female are different to a large extent because of the differences in their biological imperatives.

Extensive research has demonstrated differences between male and female across a wide range of measurement. Obviously the sexual anatomy is different, so is the reproductive function, there are marked hormonal differences, the chromosomes are different, bone structures, body size and strength differ, brain differences have been described. Sex can be determined by looking at hair under the microscope, total body fat and distribution is different, the thickness of skin differs. Psychologically, the clear difference in aggressiveness has been repeatedly observed. Intellectual differences appear at puberty. Psychological tests reveal some very fundamental differences with regard to how individuals relate to the environment. In fact, any scientific investigator who submitted a research proposal to fellow scientists would be the laughing-stock of the scientific community if he took issue with the absolute necessity to separate his subjects on the basis of sex. Distinction of research subjects on the basis of sex is probably the most fundamental step the scientist must take before proceeding with his work. Male and female simply are profoundly different—and thank Heaven for the differences! The claim that women are the way they are because of age-old discrimination is nonsense.[11]

Societies have evolved in such a way as to permit a comfortable articulation between the psychological qualities of the man and woman and their biological underpinnings. There are, to be sure, areas of overlap between men and women. Men and women do share certain physical and psychological qualities and, indeed, there are tasks in life to which either sex can adapt and which either sex can master, and where they can, they should be rewarded equally. Most people believe the equal pay for equal work concept is proper. I certainly do.

Society recognizes these shared propensities and capabilities and has opened the door wide to both sexes in many areas of life. This is as it should be. There are, however, substantial differences between male and female, and society must provide for these differences, capitalize on them, and reward them wisely. Not only does the individual find peace of mind and fulfillment when he finds his proper fit in the environment, but society gets the most out of the individual. Obviously society must also provide for a continual source of new life which can fully express itself and breathe life into the values, customs, laws, traditions, etc. which define the society and move it forward. This source of new life is, and can only be, the family. Clearly therefore, a large proportion of individuals of any society must be able to create new life and launch it well, that is to say, we *must see to it* that most of our citizens have the capacity to make families and be good parents. This is a fundamental, inescapable requirement for a society to survive, and especially for it to flourish.

When children do not receive parenting from a masculine father and feminine mother who are firmly bonded together—that is, when they do not grow up within a healthy family—their own effectiveness is inevitably weakened and their psychological identity may become blurred. In extreme cases, some individuals emerge with a psychologic identity of the opposite sex. Everyone can easily recognize an effeminate male and a masculine female. Inevitably a price is paid for these deviations. These individuals always lack the effectiveness they might have had, even though they might excel in a particular aspect of life. The hostility and competitiveness between the sexes, along with role blurring and identity confusion, which is the result of disturbed childhood development, cost both the individual and society heavily. Those who manage to enter into heterosexual relationships cannot do so with maximal effectiveness. In other words, the capacity to bond with a member of the opposite sex is weakened. This results in divorce, strained marriages, infidelity, living together outside of formal marriage, and so on and an *impaired capacity to be a parent.*

Men who are psychologically troubled have an easy way out from their family responsibilities for society has always expected the male to man the work force. The psychologically troubled male does not need a "liberation" movement; society provides one for him. Married men get away from their family responsibilities by going to work every day, and often the great dedication men show for their work is also a disguised means for escaping from family responsibilities which they cannot master because of psychological disturbances within. These disturbances generally lie relatively dormant as long as they are not triggered by too close a relationship with their wives or children.

Psychologically troubled women similarly have to get away from (be liberated from) homemaking and maternal responsibilities when their psychologic conflicts are activated by these responsibilities or the prospect of marriage. This is what the term "liberation" really refers to. Obviously these women have to do something with their lives and they do. Some never marry, some live with men (or women), some marry and never have children; some marry, become mothers and promptly go to work outside the home; some remain at home and develop some form of manifest psychiatric illness. Some become the militant champions of the women's liberation movement and impose their value system on the banner of that movement. Emotionally healthy women whose finances are adequate generally remain at home and provide the highest possible gift to the child— mothering, at least until the child starts going to school. She and her husband provide healthy family life which prepares the young for the next cycle. There are, of course, many psychologically healthy men and women who elect, for one reason or another, not to marry and become parents.

While it is true that vast numbers of women with children are forced to go to work out of financial necessity and that many gifted and skilled and trained women quite naturally return to work after their children have started school, I believe a major element of the women's liberation movement derives from another source. As I commented earlier, I am fully aware of genuine inequities which also are a motivating force in this movement. These inequities, like all injustices, should be corrected.

The statement of one of the militant women liberationists—I did not use the term feminist because I do not see true feminity within the extreme and militant elements of that movement—quoted earlier, captures a major motivation behind the movement. "We are becoming the men we wanted to marry" makes glaringly obvious the so-called "masculinity complex" in the banner of the Women's Liberation movement. This complex and its corollary, the "antifeminity complex," as manifested by those feminine women who are too anxious or timid to fulfill themselves within the context of a family of their own, are the products of developmental disturbances during childhood. These women have little choice but to alter society's values and its fabric so as to find a comfortable niche for themselves in the environment. Do not hear me as being critical of them; they are doing what they have to do.

These women (and their male counterparts who abandon their family responsibilities) are the product of several generations of disturbed family life. They are a reflection of the trend that began about seventy-five years ago. They did not receive the quality (or quantity) of parenting necessary to make it possible for them to live in harmony with a member of the opposite sex and create a family. This fact is *not their fault* nor is it the fault of their parents, or their grandparents. All were caught in a complex of social and individual interactions which disturbed their psychological development as children. They did the best they could and passed on their qualities to their children, and so on. But here is the grave danger for the future of society. When the number of these individuals is sufficiently large, society will collapse simply because too few real families exist. A species of animal life reaches extinction long before its last member dies.

The inequities for women will eventually be corrected without this faction within the Women's Liberation movement, just as inequities among men have been eliminated throughout our history and are still being addressed. The feminists' insistence that reference to sexual differences be removed from school books, government regulations, etc., their obvious quest for the man's way of life rather than enhancement of what females do best, their promotion of so-called assertive groups (which in truth teach competition rather than harmony between the sexes), their open acceptance of the lesbian influence, etc., are the unfortunate aspects of the Women's Liberation movement. These elements within the movement are expressions of the psychopathology which I have been describing. The consequences of these psychopathological elements within the women's movement are highly destructive. This faction is having its way, and our male lawmakers tremble in their presence like small boys facing a wrathful mother.

In addition to the destructive effects on the family, the next most serious aspect of the Women's Liberation movement is its success in forcing society to place women in positions which men can fill better. As a result of the misapplication of the fine concept of equal opportunity, heavy industry and industry generally are being forced, often through work quotas, to place women in positions which men can clearly do better. Managers and executives no longer have the freedom to hire the person who can do the job best. Instead of keeping the sexes separate in certain close and continuous work situations, when such close proximity distracts both sexes, the sexes are mixed with complete disregard for the powerful instinctual forces which attract male and female.

In the military, women are moving progressively toward combat responsibilities. Men and women are billeted together. Pregnant servicewomen are no longer discharged. Women are used as drill sergeants for male recruits. This is particularly alarming, for many of these young boys have never had fathers or adequate fathering, and at this highly formative period in their lives they need a father figure, not only to teach them about military life but with whom to identify. The Marines, to their great credit, do not use women as drill instructors for their recruits and they train women recruits separately.[12] The service academies admit women, and the ROTC programs mix the sexes. It would be far wiser to have a separate academy for officer training for women rather than force the women to try to behave like men (which they admit they do) so they can better integrate themselves into academy life.

All of these alterations in our way of life reinforce the trend toward unisexism and mediocrity, and contribute to the leveling process in our country. Whenever an individual cannot fill the place where his talents and abilities are best expressed, efficiency drops. Mixing the sexes as if they were equals in all respects will lower the efficiency of the particular organization. Society must reappraise the value of what women do best, upgrade the rewards and encourage the woman to develop her femininity and associated skills rather than reward her quest for the male identity and role. Furthermore, the mixing of the sexes in close quarters for prolonged periods of time disrupts male-male bonding and often creates new liaisons between male and female which disrupt the family commitment to which each should remain faithful. Sailors' wives do not like it one bit that women are going to sea with their men. They understand human nature.

Women are being forced out of the home by the ravages of inflation; others are being lured away by the false values of the Women's Liberation movement which proclaims doing your own thing outside the home is paramount in importance. Like it or not, the movement both implicitly and explicitly espouses competition and rivalry between the sexes. Many men see an easy way out from under their responsibilities and are willing to let women have it all, failing to recognize their own self-defeat and irresponsibility in so doing. Lost in this massive reordering of our way of life is the basic truth that children must have parents. Elements within various mental health professional groups and a variety of self-appointed experts are proclaiming that almost any cluster of individuals qualifies as a family, that caretaker arrangements are as good as family life. Fundamental truths about the human condition are being blindly pushed aside.

Current laws provide equal opportunity for women, as well as certain guaranteed rights and protection. These special provisions for the woman must not be lost, for to permit further erosion of the legal structure which protects women and which supports the family will surely sound the death knell for the family and society. The consequences of the Equal Rights Amendment at the level of how we live our lives is that men and women will be judged to be equivalent in all respects. Evidence abounds to brand such equivalence as a misunderstanding of the equal rights concept. Some of the most glaring examples are the proposed drafting of women into the armed forces, work quotas for women in heavy industry, the removal of any reference to sex in government regulations, guidelines, etc. On the humorous side, we read with increasing frequency of such absurdities as a court ruling that girls must be permitted to try out for boys' football teams and that girl cheerleaders be provided a steak dinner like the boys after the football game!!

The achievement of excellence and high productive efficiency depends on the freedom for the individual and for those with organizational responsibility to be discriminating in their judgments and decisions. To recognize differences in people in no way violates our democratic principles. There are tasks only women can do best and certain ones men can do best. There is nothing wrong with the separation of the sexes under certain circumstances; not to separate them can spell disaster. Obviously not all men are equal in ability, nor are all women, nor are men and women equivalent. How society rewards differences in people is a complex issue. There is where injustice exists. In the Israeli kubbutzim the unisex concept is dying out as women freely select the tasks which women traditionally enjoy doing and do best. They never again plan to use women in combat, nor do the Russians.

The United States is the only nation on earth which is seriously considering placing women in combat roles in the Armed Forces. This phenomenon like the rampant success of pornography as an industry is another glaring barometer of how far we have slipped as a society. Our potential adversaries must be jumping with glee as they witness the once mighty United States permit women to permeate our Armed Forces in areas where men function much more effectively. What more obvious indicator could there be of the softening of our national character and will?

The simple truth is that even when socially conditioned to compete athletically with either sex, females nonetheless, if left alone, avoid contact sports. This is so because of the *biologic* differences between male and female. Watch the play of a group of little girls and a group of little boys, and you can see immediately how different boys and girls are. The winning of war depends on raw, controlled vicious aggression and physical strength. Men, not women, will win wars, because they have more of these qualities. Furthermore, the fighting arm of the military organization must be fine-tuned and highly mobile and efficient. Placing women among men would be highly disruptive.

The Women's Liberation movement has thrust women into areas of work where bonding and cooperation among men is essential to the most efficient and effective carrying out of a particular task or function. Male-male bonding is a socializing force which binds large numbers of men together in a common cause or purpose.[13] Examples range from social organizations to work forces of various kinds to the Armed Forces.

Placing women among men disrupts this bonding, the more so when the members are in close quarters for prolonged periods of time. This is so because the male-female bond is very powerful, and it is private, possessive and is jealously guarded. Men will not keep their minds on their common task with women in their presence nearly as well as when there are no women present.

The male is by nature protective of the female and

all the more so when he loves a particular female. Men would unnecessarily expose themselves to the hazards of war in their efforts to protect the fighting women in their midst. I have had Viet Nam veterans tell me of their great horror when they discovered they had killed an enemy woman. The guilt eats away at them. Even though the woman was an enemy, killing her violated a powerful natural force within the male viz., to protect the female. Anticipating the harm that might come to their female comrades would place the men in a constant state of added strain and cause them to disregard their own safety to some degree, and probably totally, at crucial moments.

That the men would be distracted because of their sexual attraction can be illustrated by two anecdotes. An Army woman in training with the men was injured and sent to the hospital. She received *forty* single roses from the men in her unit. A naval officer reported that during a landing exercise, he noticed that the *entire* group of men had their eyes trained on a woman who was at the tiller. He said, "As she was spinning the wheel around her fanny was oscillating back and forth; *all* my men had their eyes on her instead of attending to last minute preparations for landing. That is when I decided women do not belong in combat or aboard ship."

Obviously the work force of society will mix the sexes to some degree—this is inevitable, necessary, and not all bad by any means. However, there are situations where the sexes should be kept separate. The feminists want women to have carte blanche access to all aspects of life. This is a mistake—just as it is a mistake for men to want to intrude totally into the woman's world.

There *are* tasks which men do better than women and vice versa. The most obvious basis for separating the sexes with regard to tasks to be performed is physical strength. The simple truth is that on the average, men are stronger than women. Women are about 60% as strong as men, and even if they are of equal weight, the woman is about 20% less powerful. Forcing heavy industry to hire a certain quota of women is wrong. To do so will eventually lower the efficiency of the particular industry. While equal opportunity is a fine guiding concept, unequal ability (in this instance, based on physical strength) is a fact of life. This fact cannot be ignored, but the feminists insist that society ignore it, and they are having their way. The cost to society is enormous.

Women are taught to be competitive and hostile toward men. Competition in the business world, the market place, etc. is a fact of life, but within the bounds of the heterosexual relationship, and certainly within the family the sexes must be in harmony. The prevailing attitude of the moment is for women to square off against men, compete with them, point to them as exploiters who demean women. This philosophy inevitably carries over into the home. The sexes should make love, not war!

Society is obligated to treat women in the work force fairly, to give them an equal opportunity to demonstrate their abilities. This principle should hold true for everyone. Society is making a fundamental error, however, when it *forces* society to make accommodations for the deficiencies in people, women in particular (since this is the focus at the moment), who are attempting to function in areas where men outperform women. In a company, for instance, special provisions have to be made for the women, not to mention the fact that they cannot perform as well at the work task itself. In the service academies—West Point, for instance—the physical standards have had to be substantially lowered. A male who functioned at the standards set for women would be dropped. Furthermore, these same women are not as usable in the Armed Forces as are men. To train them there is a waste of taxpayers' money. The women should be trained elsewhere for tasks they can do.

Sometimes a photograph or a visual image captures the essence of what is happening far better than a highly controlled (well-designed) research study. Look at a photo of various scenes of training at West Point. There you see those fine strong men performing well—and mixed among them are women—smaller in size, thinner arms, narrower shoulders, broad hips, and milder in appearance—trying desperately to emulate the hard masculine qualities of the men, but failing miserably to do so. She is a dilutant, her presence weakens the training of the Officer Corps—it is inevitable. Mix wine with beer and you have something revolting—either taken separately can be tasty and refreshing.

The solution on the broad social level is for the equal opportunity concept to remain in force, but for the government to keep hands off and permit managers and executives to have the freedom to hire the best suited person (regardless of sex, race, or religion) for the particular job. The term "best suited" will inevitably mean a person is not well-suited at times because of his sex. The American way of life emerged because we had the freedom to make choices, the freedom to find the place where we could perform best. To be discriminating in judgment is not to be discriminatory or prejudicial.

For instance, universities are being *forced* to distribute athletic funds to women under Title IX. If there is a sufficient number of women to build various kinds of teams, well and good. However, the public should not be forced to buy tickets to watch the women. Let the women compete for the public's interest, attention, and money. If they play well enough for the public to want to buy tickets to watch them, the public will buy them. No woman would ever be seen in the sports arenas if she competed against men, and if men overcame their protectiveness and gallantry toward women and competed against women as they do against other men. Women simply cannot make it; they would lose out.

In the work force where productive efficiency is a major element in the vitality of a nation, legislation is destructive which fails to recognize the differences between men and women and which ties the hands or intimidates executives and managers so they are forced to select employees who cannot function best.

America must wake up soon, or we will so cripple our social system that other nations will outperform us. My advice to men is to go out into the work force and compete against women just as if they were men. Do not be so chivalrous and gallant. Remember your job is at stake. To managers and executives my advice is to select the best person for the job and if you are accused of being discriminatory against women prove in court that you are not. To take a stand, make your case, and put up a fight. You are basically fighting *for* your country. If a woman can do the task best, then hire her, of course. Where mixing the sexes lowers efficiency, then they should not be mixed; either hire all women or all men depending on the nature of the work to be done.

When men assert themselves in the work force, women who have intruded into areas where men function better will be forced out. They will then seek jobs which they can do better than men, or equally as well. Furthermore, when men behave more assertively and responsibly, some women will be happy to return to the home, inflation permitting. If men would be men, more women would be women, and the solidity of the family would be reestablished. This in turn would improve childhood development, and these healthier children would ring out the destructive elements of the Womens Liberation movement.

The simple truth is that there are only so many jobs that pay a sufficiently high wage for a family man to provide for his family and himself. This man must out-compete all others so he gets his job or society must give priority to the family man or single parent (of either sex).

Three conditions must be met for the family to survive: (1) The man and woman must both be emotionally healthy enough to be able to make a family; (2) Society must provide a sufficient number of positions which pay enough for married men to provide for their families; and (3) Society must upgrade the recognition of the couple who make a family, in particular the woman so that her sense of worth is reinforced by factors other than those from within her family, e.g., the joy of watching her children develop well, praise from her husband, and so on.

It is imperative that society address the issue of women in the work force, find fulfilling and rewarding places for her there, but *not* at the expense of family life. Based on my observations of women for thirty years, I believe society will be astounded by how willing they are to make the family their primary career if men will be responsible and give them the security to do so, *and* if society will recognize their enormous value. No finer expressions of generosity, patience, devotion, care, dedication, and many more fine human qualities can be found than those which are demonstrated by mature women who gave us our life, nurtured us, and launched us into society.

Chapter VII
Unisexism

Today we are seeing the character of men and women change very drastically from the clearly established male and female identities of times past toward unisexism or downright role reversal. The increase in homosexuality is part of this trend. Fortunately some men and women have escaped it, but many have not, and I believe the trend will worsen before it gets better *if* it ever does. If the trend continues, our society is doomed for sexual identity blurring always weakens the durability of the male-female bond and the capacity to form a family.

Imposing the unisex values on developing children is harmful to them, yet that is exactly what is happening in America today. This is probably one of the most destructive influences of our times on our children and young adults. In schools at all levels "experts" in sociology, psychology, and even some biologists are taking the position that the differences between the sexes have been overemphasized. The textbooks of small children are being rewritten so as to obscure and even erase references to boy and girl and role preferences which the sexes have found congenial in times past.

The federal government is eliminating references

to male and female in government regulations, directives, and guidelines. Schools that receive federal aid are prohibited from restricting females from certain male activities, mostly sports. The Armed Forces are being forced to permit women to enter many areas of activity that men have exclusively occupied. The Labor Department has decreed quotas for women in heavy industry. All of these events are happening under the guiding concept of the equal right and equal opportunity acts. The capstone for blurring *any* distinction between the sexes insofar as the places they will occupy in society is the Equal Rights Amendment. This trend all adds up to the point of view that a man and woman are virtually interchangable in context, that there is no difference between male and female.

The fact of the matter is that there are enormous differences between male and female by all the methods of analysis and measurement including the most obvious—simple, direct observation. In the course of evolution, male and female have gotten progressively more differentiated. At progressively lower levels within the animal kingdom the differences between male and female are less obvious.

Differences exist between male and female in their anatomy, in the cells, in the hormones, in their chromosones, in their tissues, in how they metabolize food, and in their mental makeup. In doing research of *any kind* the most fundamental control that must be introduced in the design of the research is the separation of subjects to be studied on the basis of sex. Psychological tests in particular must control for sex.

Men and women and boys and girls are more susceptible to different diseases. On the average, women are 40% less physically strong than men. Women relate to babies and children entirely differently than do men; not to be overlooked is the fact that women have babies, and have breasts with which to nurse them, and the temperament to find these experiences profoundly satisfying. Maternalism and paternalism are different human qualities.

Yet despite these profound and extensive differences between male and female our society has gotten to the point that our young are being taught that they are not different (male vs. female), and that sexual identity and sexual role preference has been forced upon our forebears, and on them through a process of social conditioning designed by men primarily for the exploitation of women.

Not many years ago a Russian scientist imposed the Communist doctrine (which claims we are what we are because of social influences) on his botanical research. Unfortunately for him, but fortunately for the rest of us, the laws of Nature were powerful enough to withstand his tinkering, and he was proven to be a fraud. In time, unisexists, sociologists, psychologists, etc. who peddle the unisex line which claims women have been conditioned to their position in life by evil male chauvinists will be just as roundly discredited.

While the human intellect or spirit enjoys great plasticity and is highly adaptive, it is sheer blindness to fail to see the connection between our mind and our body. The quality of a tree and a bush is different because of their structural differences. A rose is a rose and not a daisy because of the wide range of structural differences that appear with every type of measurement and analysis. The overall differences between male and female are best described by poets and artists; the individual differences are as profound as they are necessary and can be demonstrated scientifically.

In addition to the differences between the sexes there are a wide range of differences between individuals within each sex. Every parent, in particular the mother, will tell you each of her children was different at birth. The art of parenting is to detect the differences in babies and foster the unfolding of the great potential that lies dormant in their biology. No potential is of more profound importance than the child's maleness or femaleness. No single environmental influence does more damage to the developing human spirit than[14] to impose the wrong psychological sexual identity on the biological imperative of the child.

The key to a successful life is to be fortunate enough to have had parents and others evoke and develop your potential. Ultimately, each individual must be psychologically in harmony with what he is biologically, and then find a harmonious fit with the environment. No aspect of this intricate and complex process is more important than for the infant and child to receive the kind of mothering and fathering that leads to maleness or femaleness in the male and female, and to ultimately find a social role which permits the full expression of those very different psychological qualities.

It is true, because of man's adaptability, that the individual can force himself to *behave* in ways that are not in harmony with his basic qualities. To do so always produces strain that damages both the psychology and physiology of the individual. A male who is forced by his childhood development to acquire the psychological identity of a female and live out that identity is in a profound state of internal conflict. The same applies to the female. Similarly, men and women whose psychology is in harmony with their biology, but who are forced by necessity or social pressure to live out a social role which is contrary to their basic makeup produces conflict and strain. The social revolution in which we are all caught up is taking its toll.

There is no more sure way for parents and others to impair the psychological development of children than to effeminize boys and to masculinize girls. Powerful social forces are at work, however, which push parents in that direction. Work guidelines, social legislation, textbooks, clothing, and hair styles favor unisexism and not sexual differentiation. Parents, I urge you to reject these trends. Rear your children so that your little girl becomes a woman and your little boy becomes a man. Only then will they *not* be in conflict with themselves and with members of the opposite sex. Nothing in the human condition and experience is more fundamental than becoming psychologically what you are biologically.

People who are not in conflict psychologically, and this also means they are not in conflict with what they are biologically, usually manage to find a place for themselves in society if they are given the freedom to do so. Great social pressure exists today which in effect robs young men and women of their freedom of choice. The impact of laws such as Title IX or the Equal Opportunity Act which provide for freedom of choice on the young is vastly different than social movements which use these laws to further their own aims. The effect on young women and on society of the freedom for women to enter heavy industry is very different from social pressure which proclaim that true "personhood" can only be found if women enter these fields of endeavor.

Unfortunately social pressure and even governmental intervention (through mandatory work quotas, for instance) do exist which impinge on young women (in particular) to seek ways of living which they might otherwise not seek if they followed their inner (truer) inclinations. There are many males who would not let their hair grow long if they were not influenced by social trends.

The great economic growth of America resulted from the freedom for the economic laws to be expressed. The same applies to human growth and potential. Individuals must have the freedom to develop within the family *and* have the freedom to find the right place for themselves in society. That freedom must be protected by law.

Chapter VIII

The "Normalization" of Homosexuality

I have already pointed out the lowered capacity of increasing numbers of people (as reflected in the divorce rate and other statistics) to make the heterosexual bond durable. This trend is entirely predictable in light of the severe disturbances within the family life of the developing young. The sexual drive is a fundamental element in human nature; so too is the need for closeness with other human beings. Homosexuals have these needs and drives too, but they are so filled with irrational fear and guilt having to do with intimacy with a member of the opposite sex that they turn to a member of the same sex for the gratification of their needs. Statistics suggest that homosexuality is increasing; its visibility certainly is. A spokesman for the homosexuals claims there are 25 million of them in the United States. Reputedly one-fourth of the residents of San Francisco are homosexual. The large Western seaboard cities attract them as do most large cities.

Dr. Abram Kardiner, a distinguished physician, psychoanalyst, and anthropologist, has stated that homosexuality reaches an epidemic level in societies which are in crisis or in a state of collapse.[15] The fact

90 Families

that homosexuals are coming "out of the closet" in droves, and are agitating for free access to all aspects of society is an ominous sign indeed. Even more ominous is the fact that a number of powerful mental health organizations have placed what amounts to a stamp of normality on this condition and have endorsed many of their social objectives.[16]

The increase in numbers of homosexuals and the increasing inclination of society to open all doors to them and even to define their psychological sickness as normal is one of the many manifestations of the disintegration of our society. Do not be fooled by homosexual propaganda which claims we are in an age of enlightenment, that the condition is merely a variation of normality.

I am frequently asked the question "What is wrong with permitting homosexuals to participate in all aspects of society and, further, who is to say their way of life is not normal? After all, haven't there always been homosexuals, including some very great people? And further, what difference does it make what people do in private?"

Before answering those questions, the true nature of the condition should first be discussed.

A fundamental question regarding human nature is whether man is biologically bisexual. Solid evidence strongly suggests he is not. Until about seven weeks, the human embryo is bipotential, but then events take place which cause the embryo to develop along existing lines and become female or change its direction and become male. Furthermore, a historical perspective of man's evolution shows unmistakably that evolution from the single cell to man has been in the direction of ever greater sexual differentiation, and not toward androgny or unisexism. To be sure, men and women have some common component parts, and common characteristics, but when the sum of the parts is added up, the "wholes" (male and female) are strikingly different. A child is born with enormous potential locked in his biology. Life experience unlocks this potential and develops it. None is more fundamental than that which leads to gender identity. Good parenting accomplishes this development.

Animals do not display true homosexual behavior. They do occasionally show displacement behavior, that is, they will at times mount (but not penetrate) a member of the same sex, but this does not occur when a sexually receptive female is available. Displacement behavior is nothing more than seeking out an object onto which to express a drive or impulse or motivation when the drive-specific object is not available. Homosexuals displace their sexual drives onto members of the same sex *not* because of the unavailability of the opposite sex but because *severe psychological conflicts* within their own minds prevent them from gratifying their sexual needs and need for interpersonal closeness with a member of the opposite sex to a completely satisfying degree.

Much publicity was recently given to apparent homosexuality among seagulls and naturally the gays and some professionals made much of this. Further study, however, showed that there was a shortage of the opposite sex among these gulls. Nature was compelling them to live out the mating instinct even though a suitable mate did not exist. Such animal behavior does not demonstrate fundamental homosexuality in man. Another study of 10 thousand seagulls on Long Island failed to find a single incident of 'homosexuality'.[17] Quite predictably, an even number of male and female seagulls existed in this study.

If homosexuality reflected a fundamental bisexuality then it should appear in all cultures. It does not, and furthermore, its prevalence is much greater in highly advanced societies where family life suffers greater disturbances. The condition is unknown among the Ute and Apache Indians, in the aborigines, and in some tribes in Africa.

Hormonal studies do not correlate with the condition. Occasionally a report appears where the male hormone level is lower in the homosexual group (*vs.* heterosexual), but these reports are rare. Even if such reports were common, the field of psychosomatic medicine could easily explain the finding. We know that psychological conflicts and the emotions can have powerful effects on physiological processes, even on life itself. It would come as no surprise if homosexuals had lower male hormone levels, but most studies show they do not.

Twin studies do not exist where identical twins were separated at birth and reared by different parents where these twins nonetheless *both* became homosexual. That there is greater homosexuality in identical twins in contrast to non-identical twins reared by the same parents proves nothing. The common pattern is for one child among several siblings to become homosexual. Since identical twins are generally the same, it follows logically that both should become homosexual.

It is very interesting to note that not all identical twins show a high concordance of homosexuality. More often, one of the twins is homosexual and the other is not.[18] When the family patterns are looked into, it has been found that the male homosexual member of the twin pair (these are male twins) was the mother's favorite while the heterosexual twin counterpart was emotionally closer to the father. These facts provide powerful additional support for the view that homosexuality is not caused by biologic factors. This study is entirely consistent with the work of Beiber.[19]

Chromosonal studies do not reveal differences in heterosexuals and homosexuals, and it is highly unlikely that differences will appear in the molecular configuration of the genes (RNA and DNA). Even if differences should appear, such a finding could hardly place the stamp of normality on homosexuality. Some of man's most severe illnesses are caused by biological disturbances, cancer in particular. Sickle cell anemia is another example.

Finally, homosexuality is treatable by psychological methods when the treating person is knowledgeable about the human condition, is skilled in certain psychotherapeutic techniques, and *if* if his own personality is free from certain personality disturbances. Obviously, a homosexual doctor would have difficulty helping a patient resolve the psychological conflicts which lead to his homosexuality because of the

94 *Families*

doctor's own psychological conflicts *and* his belief that homosexuality is normal.

Homosexuality is caused by the nature of the parents' interaction with the developing infant and child. This process is profoundly influenced by the personalities of both parents and the nature of their relationship with each other. The data which have been collected by doctors who do in-depth (psychoanalytic) studies of people for the purpose of helping them overcome their disturbance are entirely consistent with studies of the family patterns of homosexuals. The so-called "close binding" mother or the anxious or hostile mother and the absent or remote and hostile father causes the boy to never develop properly. Instead he develops severe emotional conflicts which prevent him from becoming a self-confident male who can experience loving and sexual feelings toward a woman. Little girls go through a comparable development; however, often their fathers were much too close to them. Excellent books and articles exist which describe the nature of this condition.[20]

My purpose in devoting a chapter to this condition is to suggest that the increase in the number of homosexuals and their aggressive social movement, the aim of which is to gain access to all aspects of society *and* to have their way of life defined as normal is another (and very ominous) sign of the deterioration of our society. Their movement reflects a "normalization" of human qualities and a way of life which is one of the most severe disturbances of the human condition. The most obvious justification for that statement is the fact that *if* all people (and lower forms of animal life) were homosexual the animal kingdom would cease to exist. Furthermore, studies into the minds of homosexuals reveal the presence of profound conflicts which not only explain the condition, but lead indisputably to the definition of psychopathology. Now, to return to the questions asked earlier.

All cultures, including ancient Greece and Rome, place and have placed severe limitations on homosexual behavior when it existed in their culture. Biblical writers have done so also. The reason for this universal stance is obvious. To define the condition as normal permits a way of life to become part of the social fabric and to have a destructive feedback effect on individuals as well as social processes. Sick or destructive ways of behaving are prohibited or downgraded by customs, traditions, and laws in order to protect and stabilize society.

Today our own society is struggling with the issue of how far it will go in permitting homosexuals to permeate society, e.g., the classroom, the mental health profession, Armed Forces, "marriage," etc. Obviously, homosexuals have a right to live in the society that created them. However, I do not believe they should be permitted to occupy any social position of their choice.

This same principle applies to all individuals. There are places where we fit or belong and can contribute to society in a constructive manner and there are places where we cannot. This fact is obvious. The issue of homosexuals in the classroom as teachers is a hot issue currently. If the premise is accepted that children on up through junior high level and even high school level should be exposed to the most healthy (emotionally) individuals possible, then homosexuals should be excluded from the teaching profession at least to the high school level. Obviously, many emotionally disturbed heterosexuals should be excluded as well. Young children should be exposed to the healthiest adults possible. For some children their school teacher is the healthiest person who will have an impact on their developing personalities.

The homosexuals are making a grave mistake by attempting to "sell" society on the notion that theirs is a normal condition or one that is freely chosen and that they should have free access to all aspects of society. They would, in the long run, be far less ostracized, and perhaps not at all, if they admitted they are emotionally disturbed and asked society to show compassion for them and assimilate them into society where their sickness would not adversely affect the young or emotionally vulnerable. What appears to be discrimination against homosexuals is society's way of insuring itself against the feedback destructive impact of a sick condition which disturbs family life.

Homosexuals are emotionally sick people. If a society incorporates this way of life into its basic structure, it too becomes a sicker society and therefore and inevitably a weakened one. Since gender identity, that is, what defines a male and female is at the very heart of the cultural revolution which is sweeping through our nation, it is imperative that strong and healthy people take a stand against the gay propagandists. It is equally imperative for vulnerable heterosexuals to not be tipped into the homosexual world for their own personal welfare and for the best interests of society.

If you learn that your son or daughter is homosexual, you should face it squarely. Do not panic, and above all, do not reject your child. To do so will almost surely consolidate the homosexual condition. Many who are homosexual will simply flatly refuse offers of help, but make the offer nonetheless. Try to find a professional person who is expert in this area of psychopathology and obtain help for your child. Do not give up if you don't find help immediately. Our society sorely needs treatment centers for homosexuals, but until the day arrives when such centers exist, individuals will have to seek help on their own through private sources. Help does exist, not enough to treat all, but some at least. The most enlightened and determined individuals will be able to find that help.

To ignore your child's homosexuality, or to try to convince yourself that the condition is normal is nothing more than a way to deny your part in his emotional development and of course, this is the strategy of the gay community; call the condition normal so they do not have to do anything about it.

Chapter IX

Pornography: A Barometer of the Nation's Sickness

Pornography in its various forms is a multibillion dollar business in the United States. Pornography depicts all of the perversions and debases women in the worst possible way. This business flourishes because of its appeal to millions of Americans. The simple curiosity of emotionally healthy people would never support the ever-expanding pornography industry. This business is a shocking and ominous barometer of the state of emotional health of millions of our fellow citizens. It confirms the institutionalization of psychopathology. Worse, our laws and lawmakers, whose function and duty it is to maintain the best values of society, are slowly but surely yielding to the impact of the ever-increasing mass of sickness which has found expression in this particular form. The federal courts' application of the principle of community standards with regard to what is obscene, beautifully illustrates how human psychopathology eventually permeates the values of society—in this instance with the blessing of the courts.

In addition to outright pornography, the open display of near-explicit sex appears everywhere. It is difficult to watch television without observing many references to sex and, of course, violence too. There appear to be as many "R" rated movies as those rated suitable for the young. Our society has relaxed its constraint on sexuality so extensively that the senses are dulled to these stimuli. However, the consequences for society are profound. Illegitimate births are soaring and pregnancy among teenagers is at an epidemic level. The consequences of all of this are downright tragic. Sex has become a part of even the most casual relationships. Less obvious but equally serious is the overall lowering of cultural excellence within our country. It has been repeatedly observed that there is an inverse relationship between sexual license and the cultural excellence. That is to say, the sexual drive is a force within the creative process. When most of the sexual energy of a society is expressed directly as raw sex, less of its energy finds its way into the creative process.

Sexual expression between mature couples who have a meaningful relationship adds depth to life. One can dine well or degenerate into gluttony. The same applies to sex. When the social pattern tilts toward sexual gluttony, the culture will trend toward decline. This is happening in our country.

The unbridled sexual expression of today and the flourishing pornography business are a direct outgrowth of the breakdown of family life. I will describe this relationship in this chapter, and thereby demonstrate again how very sick our society has become. It is inevitable that broken, strained, or part-time families will lead to disturbed personality development and that those disturbances will lead to a breakdown of rational constraints on sexuality, to rampant pornography, and to an overall cultural decline. Follow the steps of this chapter and you will understand how this happens.

In order to best understand the origin of pornography and how pornography in turn influences the individual and society, it is necessary to explain the appeal of pornography, that is, to explain what it is in people that makes them produce and view such material and how their actions stem from disturbed family life.

The strength and permanence of the heterosexual bond, the commitment between a man and a woman within the institution of the family, directly determines the outcome of the psychological development of the children they produce. In order for a man and woman to attain a high level of commitment, their own personalities must be relatively free from emotional conflicts and psychopathology. The more complete the sense of maleness and femaleness the couple has achieved, the more harmonious their relationship will be. The healthiest children are produced by mature, masculine men and mature, feminine women who deeply love each other and whose family life has not been disrupted by the cruel hand of fate.

The underpinning of personality is biologic. One aspect of human biology which has a profound effect on the emerging psychological side of personality is an instinctual force, the gratification of which brings the child great pleasure. This instinctual energy is intimately connected with fundamental bodily functions. These instinctual forces also become attached to the parents in differing ways as the child undergoes personality development. These instinctual gratifications and early attachments are at the heart of the appeal of pornography; they are the basis for the so-called prurient appeal.

Pornography depicts these primitive instinctual gratifications and, in so doing, excites residual developmental immaturities which exist *to some degree* in all individuals. Pornography therefore appeals to the immature, the retrogressive elements in personality, and therefore has a destructive impact on the individual. Naturally some individuals are far more vulnerable to pornography than others. These are the people whose childhood development did not proceed well because of disturbances within their family, or because of broken families. The residue of incomplete instinctual and personality development is greater in them than in those who are more fully matured.

The first instinctual gratification of the child is largely oral in nature. The nursing experience is profoundly gratifying to the infant, not just because of the satiation of hunger, but because of the tactile sensations of the mouth and the experience of sucking. This simple and natural process is associated with the mothering function which forms the core of personality. Through good mothering and abundant and satisfying oral gratification, the child develops an inner sense of goodness, courage, and the capacity to trust. These early months are exceedingly important. When the child achieves his full measure of mothering, he proceeds to subsequent developmental stages.

A child may, however, experience serious so-called oral fixations if these early months of life are frustrating or prematurely interrupted. These frustrated instinctual drives are associated with life experiences, largely with the mother or mother surrogate, the totality of which lead to the formation of emotional conflicts. These conflicts are repressed into the unconscious region of the mind and there they must be dealt with in one way or another by the developing personality. A certain degree of developmental arrest is always associated with the formation of psychic conflict. As a consequence, the final personality is somewhat weakened in its overall effectiveness; symptoms may later erupt; there is always a heightened vulnerability to certain kinds of environmental situations.

Bowel and bladder functions also bring pleasure to the child. The process of learning to control these bodily functions can proceed smoothly, or it can lead to developmental conflict. These psychic conflicts also become repressed. The oral and anal functions provide a form of pleasure which fits into the overall fabric of so-called infantile sexuality.

A fact which many people have difficulty believing is that children also experience genital sensations. These sensations are associated with enormously important family processes which have a profound effect on the final configuration of the adult personality and the degree of the individual's effectiveness in life. While many may not feel comfortable with the fact, the fact remains that children do have sexual feelings. These feelings are awakened by the parent of the opposite sex and they, in turn, become the target for, or the object onto which those feelings are projected. This is a normal part of the child's personality development. The awakening of a child's genital sexuality is one of the central and inevitable functions of parenthood. This process proceeds usually without anyone's noticing it; however, the observant parent will notice these stirrings and aspirations in their children. Little girls have fantasies of marriage to father, having babies by him, and so on. In a family where the parents have no or minimal personality disturbances (which when present always produce strains in their marriage), and therefore have a solid relationship with each other, the child's erotic and romantic aspirations toward the parent eventually become substantially diminished, and in some, totally extinguished.

The boy eventually sees his father as his best friend, his ally; he is no longer the hated rival. The boy then identifies with his father. The girl similarly abandons her aspirations with her father, and she identifies with her mother. When the early instinctual life of the child is guided well by mature parents, the basic fabric of personality is formed.

The child is now prepared for an adult heterosexual relationship, and other adult responsibilities when grown. As you can see, a solid home life is essential for these developmental processes to proceed in the correct fashion. In the mature adult erotic feelings are experienced alongside love feelings. In a mature marriage, loveless sex does not exist; instead, love and sexuality are shared with the spouse.

Much can go wrong, however, during the crucial formative childhood years. In addition to developmental arrests at the so-called pregenital levels, the romantic and sexualized (Oedipal) period I just described may not be completed. Boys may remain attached to their mothers and never identify with their fathers. Girls may retain a father-fixation and may even identify with him. When this happens, the children have no way to extinguish the enormous guilt and anxiety which are associated with their erotic and romantic strivings. The guilt and anxiety are generated by the fact that the boy loves and fears his father, and wishes he were out of the way so he could have mother all to himself. The same formulations apply to the girl.

An outright broken home also places a severe handicap on the child. These conflicts cannot be resolved when one parent is gone. A weak father who is jealous of his son drives the boy ever closer to his mother rather than drawing the son closer to him and out of the romantic tie with his mother. Fathers often are much too close to their daughters. Some parents are outright seductive toward the child of the opposite sex, but are unaware of being so. Volumes have been written about these human developmental processes and their consequences. *The disturbances of childhood development provide the basis for an interest in pornography.*

Pornography depicts all of the perversions, including homosexuality, and often in their rawest form.

106   *Families*

Lacking in all of the depictions of heterosexual intercourse, regardless of style or form, is even the remotest reference to love between the man and woman. It is raw sex, usually highly perverse, and nothing else. Bowel and bladder functions are included in pornographic material and, more recently, children and animals are included in pornographic movies, pictures, and writings. Sadism and masochism, that is, the aggressive instinct, is also part of the pornographic scene. More recently, the theme of incest, usually between father and daughter, is depicted or alluded to.

A perversion is nothing more than the substitution of another mode for expressing sexual instinct rather than the genital one, or the substitution of the normal object (a member of the opposite sex) with someone or something else onto which the sexual impulse is to be released, or both. Perverse sexual behavior may show disturbance in mode and object of sexual expression. The reasons for these substitutions include those developmental fixations or arrests, to which I referred earlier, and the severe guilt and anxiety associated with childhood genital sexuality which was never extinguished. The guilt and anxiety force the sexual instinct to find expression in some way other than the genital route with a member of the opposite sex. Or, if sexual expression can take that route, it is dehumanized, nearly always degrades the woman, and is devoid of any expression of love between the participants.

Homosexuality is one of the consequences of serious childhood disturbances in psychosexual development. This is an abnormal condition, and as could be expected, homosexual X-rated movies are part of the pornographic scene.

When society sanctions the distribution of pornographic material, it is legitimizing (normalizing) psychopathology. The most glaring illustration of this process is the progress homosexuals are making in having their way of life defined as normal, even to the extent of being permitted to "marry," adopt children, and even undergo artificial insemination or have themselves made pregnant by some male. These developments are about as serious a corruption of the definition of normal family processes as I can imagine, and yet they are being "legitimized."

The fact that pornography or nearly explicit sex is displayed on the screen, on the printed page, and even on television practically without restraint is a sign of the decay of our society. The few successful prosecutions of the perpetrators of pornography are pitiful indeed. These few successes are virtually meaningless in the face of the tidal wave of the billions of dollars of profit which are made through the distribution of pornography. In order for these billions to be made, millions of Americans enjoy looking at it. What does this say about the American character?

It says just exactly what you are thinking. Increasing numbers of Americans contain substantial psychopathology within themselves and do not reach full maturity. They cannot find fulfillment in their personal lives generally and with a member of the opposite sex in particular. Instead they find gratification through pornography, or free-wheeling sexual behavior. The simple truth is that mature men and women have no interest in pornography and promiscuous sexuality. Their curiosity may lead to an inspection of pornography, but they do not generate a persistent interest in it. They do not simply because there is little in their unconscious minds to which the material can appeal. They would rather experience sex *and love* with and for their spouse, because that is where their maturity takes them.

Many people do not reach a full measure of maturity and therefore retain within themselves repressed, that is, unconscious elements from their imperfectly resolved childhood sexual conflicts. These conflicts generally lie quite dormant throughout a lifetime. Actually, everyone retains a trace of some degree of developmental conflict having to do with sexuality. In light of the high divorce rate, the high illegitimacy rate, the severe strains within many families which do remain intact, and the number of families where the mothers have gone to work before the children are in school, it is inevitable that pornography will continue to flourish and appeal to ever-greater numbers of people, and that constraints on sexuality generally will continue to decline. While another barometer is hardly needed as regards the trend our society is taking, the wide appeal of pornography tells us very clearly what is happening to the psychological health of millions of us and to the value system in which we live. Perverse sex and sex without love and commitment is part of the times. Unless this growing trend is reversed, and until the heterosexual bond is strong once again for a larger proportion of Americans, we will continue on our downward slide and may eventually see the end of the America which once led the world in almost all respects. Depraved sexuality and epidemic homosexuality are signs of a dying culture. Recall what happened in ancient Rome.

While individuals contribute to the form taken by society, society also affects the individual. In other words, while the pornography industry is the outgrowth of individual psychopathology, the industry itself has a feedback effect on individuals. It is sheer naivete to believe that pornography does not affect individuals and ultimately have a destructive effect on society generally. One does not need to look for research evidence to make this point. Consider how susceptible we all are to changes in style, in clothing, music, automobiles, etc. Many a healthy youth has tried drugs because of peer pressure. Such a youngster is far less vulnerable than the emotionally disturbed youth, but he tries it, and some get hooked. It is far easier to withstand social pressure when the appeal is to elements within your personality of which you are aware, such as curiosity, than to unconscious factors, particularly those with which pleasure is associated.

How then does pornography affect people? There are several ways.

1. The very healthy may, out of curiosity, view the material; they may even experiment a bit in their personal lives with what they saw, but soon discard it all.

110   *Families*

2. Older people whose sexual powers are declining may erroneously believe viewing pornographic material will improve their sex lives. While their excitement may be temporarily heightened, their performance will not be. More often they will not be able to equal the "performance" of those they viewed or read about, and will end up with even lower self-esteem than before. Their own performance anxiety will be heightened and their performance impaired.

3. Believing they are keeping in step with the times, a couple may introduce some of the behavior—usually clearly perverse—into their sexual pattern with each other. While it may be true that variety is the spice of life, this phrase does not apply to the variations of the sexual theme as depicted by pornography. Couples may severely offend each other through the introduction of the perversions to their sex life. A man may grow dissatisfied with his wife on the erroneous belief that just because she does not go through all the gyrations he saw on the screen, she is dull. His wife may, in fact, be capable of the deepest of feeling for him and capable of fine orgasmic response. What more could any reasonable man want? Couples are being misguided and misinformed as to what is best in man-woman relations through pornography. Imagine the effects of anal penetration on a fine woman. Can she possibly think better of herself for having permitted this? What must she think of her husband who suggested and did it? The psychological significance of the vagina and the rectum are worlds apart. Couples have di-

vorced because of the man's growing discontent with his wife because of his continual exposure to X-rated movies.

4. Young people who would otherwise work out a satisfactory and mature sexual style after they marry, nowadays carry with them a repertoire of techniques which they learned from viewing X-rated movies. In times past, and because their psychosexual development was reasonably good, they would have adhered to a more mature standard of behavior, i.e., heterosexual intercourse. Now, having been exposed to pornography, they more often try out other forms of sexual activity. To do so runs the risk of introducing immature and perverse sexual behavior into their sexual pattern and thereby induces a psychological regression. I will illustrate this with a case history further on.

5. Society is filled with increasing numbers of people who, because of their emotional conflicts, are extremely vulnerable to the effects of pornography. This is so because they come from disturbed or broken families. Their unconscious minds are filled with the conflicts I described earlier. Viewing pornographic material triggers these elements and induces less mature behavior. Once these unconscious forces have been integrated into overt behavioral patterns it is very difficult to remove them. This category of people I believe accounts for the fact that pornography has become a multibillion dollar a year industry.

A case illustration will demonstrate the conflict triggering effects of pornography on a vulnerable young man. The effects of his behavior on his new bride were profound and produced extreme changes in her personality, and nearly wrecked their marriage. In high school this young fellow appeared to be the all-American boy. He was a good student, and athlete, and he had high aspirations for the future. His family life had not been the best, however, and certain developmental disturbances were the result. On balance the healthy side of him outweighed the sick elements. In college, he began to date and promptly developed anxiety in association with his efforts to be close to his girl friends. For reasons he could not at first explain, he was drawn to X-rated movies and various pornographic publications, probably to reassure himself by feeling more familiar with sex. He soon became preoccupied with this exposure. He was attempting to overcome his anxieties about heterosexual intimacy. Not only did the movies and publications *not* help him, he picked up ideas that he had never thought of or heard of. Before long he initiated these various sexual techniques with women, avoiding frank intercourse. Eventually he managed to have intercourse, provided the young woman emulated prostitute-type behavior.

Within a few years he met a fine young woman who appealed to the healthy elements in him. They were married within a year. She entered marriage with high expectations. Her highest dream was to have a family. She was a feminine young woman who approached her wedding night fully expecting to be loved by her manly-appearing husband. She was bitterly disappointed. Within a few weeks after marriage this man began criticizing her values. He depreciated her frilly nighty. He wanted her to wear black things and garters. He performed the well-known perversions with her, including anal intercourse. She felt cheapened, degraded, and became non-orgasmic. Her feelings became totally inhibited when it became apparent that her husband felt no love whatsoever for her during his sexual activities with her.

This woman soon developed an interest in feminist literature and eventually became an ardent and militant member of that movement. Life had taught her that women *are* only sexual objects and instruments for the depraved behavior of men. This couple eventually found their way into psychiatric treatment where both made substantial changes for the better. They eventually overcame their unconscious conflicts, and the healthy aspects which had held them together grew and flourished. They eventually created a family.

The woman was astounded by the discovery in her treatment that she too had marked psychosexual disturbances within the depths of her. These had contributed to her choice of this man, even though she failed at the time to recognize this fact. Had her husband been a totally healthy, or even a healthier man, his impact on her would have been entirely different. She would not have undergone the psychologic regression and, in all likelihood, she would have matured in response to him and would never have required psychiatric help. Instead, his interest in pornography and her exposure to it induced a profound regression and a revision of her entire value system.

Had this young man not been introduced to sexual perversions and sex through pornography, his chances of maturing within the context of his marriage would have increased. The bond between the healthy elements in both of them would have induced further maturation in both through mutual reinforcement.

Another example of the illness-triggering effects of pornographic material is that of a young foreign physician who had led a correct life in a country where there was no pornography. Upon coming to this country, pornographic materials did not escape his attention. Though married to a fine young bride, he could not keep his mind off the pornographic materials, especially when he felt his wife was not meeting all of his needs. He eventually developed the pattern of going to X-rated movies, looking at pornographic publications, and masturbating. He grew distant from his wife, and eventually the marriage became deeply strained.

Perversions are difficult to treat because of the element of pleasure associated with them. Despite the fine qualities in this young doctor and despite his most sincere efforts to cooperate with his psychiatric treatment, he returned periodically to pornography at those very moments when he might be turning instead toward his wife and deepening and enriching his relationship with her. There was an addictive aspect to his preoccupation with pornography as is the case for many who regularly view it.

Those movies which depict the theme of incest are

especially damaging. The child's incestuous interest in the parent of the opposite sex is a normal aspect of childhood development. These interests should never become too intense nor last too long; normally they are more or less extinguished by the age of six years. However, as increasing numbers of families disintegrate, it is inevitable that ever-increasing numbers of children will be deprived of the opportunity to develop normally and thereby mature beyond their incestuous interests. It is no surprise that the theme of incest has found its way into pornography along with perverse sexuality, in view of the rate at which families are disintegrating. It is inevitable that these movies awaken and reinforce the unresolved incestuous conflicts of the viewer and thereby do him much harm. Overt psychiatric disturbances frequently erupt as a consequence of a single triggering experience. I shudder to think of the overt psychopathology that undoubtedly has developed in millions of vulnerable people as a consequence of viewing pornography.

Common sense tells us pornography influences the individual. My own clinical experience convinces me without any doubt. A few studies provide further support to this belief. The Surgeon General's report of 1972 shows an unmistakable link between TV violence and violent behavior in children. The Bartells' book on group sex states that couples who entered into this type of behavior attribute the onset of their behavior to pornography.[21] The article by Malamultz and Fishback states their belief that viewing pornography lifts not only the taboo on sex, but also the taboo on aggression. They believe that "viewing the erotic film, we communicate the unspoken message that taboo behavior like sex is O.K.," "Men exposed to violent pornography were more sexually aroused than others by reading the story of a rape," and "Psychologists, in our opinion, ought not support, implicitly or explicitly, the use of violent pornography."

It was inevitable that the disturbed psychosexual development of the millions of children who grew up, and continue to grow up, in less than good family circumstances, would eventually find expression in the social scene in a raw and undisguised form. The flourishing pornography business is that expression. Pornography depicts on the screen, the printed page, on television, and on the live stage, what exists in the sick personalities of millions of our fellow Americans.

When responsible adults permit this sickness to be displayed virtually without any restriction, the younger members of society believe that elders condone these forms of behavior. New values are thereby introduced into society. Abnormal sexuality which is depicted in pornographic material, and mature sexuality should, in my opinion, be recorded in two places only—in medical textbooks and other scientific papers and in true literary creations where a point is to be made about the human condition. Society and individuals alike can only be harmed when we "legitimize" psychopathology and fail to place reasonable restraints on sexuality in general. For a society to survive, it must strengthen the constructive elements within it and within people. It is the responsibility of the State, the Church, and the family to continually address this issue.

Chapter X

The Drug Epidemic

That the people of the United States are consuming more drugs than any other nation on earth is no accident. The level of consumption is at an epidemic level; we are in a crisis. Efforts to control the importation of drugs into the United States and the controls on domestically grown marijuana and the manufacture of other drugs and drug paraphernalia are ineffective. A destructive forest fire is sweeping across the nation. To hold to the belief that the drug scene will pass is sheer fantasy. To accommodate drugs into our way of life, as some suggest we do, ranks at the top of lunatic thinking. In order to function best, the human mind should be exposed only to those chemicals which participate in normal physiological processes except in instances where a clear medical need exists.

While it is true that drugs provide a quick and effortless means by which to achieve pleasure, I do not believe this fact alone explains the drug epidemic which is sweeping across America. Bear in mind that 80 to 100 billion dollars worth of profit is generated each year in our country through the sale of illicit drugs. This does not represent a mere fad, or the "in thing" to do. I believe millions of our fellow-Americans face the challenge of life with much anxiety. True individuality, which makes it possible to master the challenges and responsibilities of adolescence and adulthood without anxiety and/or depression, is the result of good home life, good parenting. Millions of our people did not receive these basic nutrients for the human spirit, and the drug epidemic is but one of the many consequences of this sad fact.

In-depth studies have shown conclusively that drugs are used initially because of psychological need.[22] That is to say, drug usage is found in those individuals who are psychologically troubled. Drugs tend to combat anxiety, anguish and depression, or they energize those who are lacking the drive to carry on in life. This was so in the past and is still so; however, because drug taking has become part of our way of life, those who might otherwise not have done so are today using drugs because of social pressure. The young are especially vulnerable to these influences, including those who come from relatively healthy families. The pleasure aspects of drug usage and peer pressure are difficult for young people to withstand.

Psychological vulnerabilities and weaknesses which lead to drug use are a product of the quality of parenting the child received during his developmental years and also a function of instability in the family. These vulnerabilities are most commonly felt by the potential drug user when faced by the responsibilities of life. Young people who are in the process of leaving home and on the threshold of assuming adult responsibilities are likely to experience various painful emotional states most acutely. Children in families which are unstable or broken are most vulnerable to the pressures from within themselves and to pressure from their environment to use drugs.[23]

All drugs have a habituating and/or addicting effect to some degree. In time, regardless of the original basis for beginning drug use, the drug itself creates a need for more drugs which severely compounds the problem. Substance abuse is a vicious trap to fall into. That millions of our fellow citizens use drugs regularly is another ominous barometer of the number of impaired personalities which inhabit our land. The depth of the drug epidemic is another measure of the disintegrative trend taking place in America.

Most who read this book are well aware that drugs are harmful. I want to share some personal, in-depth observations with you on the effects of marijuana.

My interest in marijuana was sparked by the apparent effects of the substance which seemed to be a part of the regressive or disintegrative process in a psychiatric inpatient population where its use appeared in the history and/or was part of the ongoing clinical picture. My interest became greatly intensified when I observed the pronounced changes which occurred in a number of young people, both patients and non-patients, who I knew were smoking marijuana. As the marijuana epidemic got into full swing, it was not long before a number of my younger outpatients, whom I was treating by psychotherapy, and those of my supervisees, reported that they were smoking marijuana. These latter observations provided an in-depth view of the intrapsychic vulnerabilities which increase the likelihood for drug usage and of the effects of the drugs. To provide some degree of validation for my inferences as regards the effects of the drug, I interviewed a number of school teachers, psychiatrists, and a number of young people about their own experiences and their observations of their friends who smoked marijuana.

As a result of these varied sources of information, I have concluded that marijuana is a harmful substance and that continuous usage has harmful psychic effects and eventually produces profound personality changes. Obviously some individuals are more adversely affected than others, depending on the extent of the use of the drug and unquestionably on the basic strength of personality of the user. These remarks are based on clinical and other observations, to be sure, but the evidence is so clear, at least to me, that I have no hesitation whatsoever in stating this opinion.

Among psychiatric inpatients I noticed that a disheveled appearance is rather common. Their life adjustment had been very poor. Many were drifters, or were unable to work at all. Their personal lives had failed in most respects. Their marriages collapsed, they abandoned their responsibilities. In some cases it was not possible to precisely identify when marijuana had become part of the disintegrative picture. Undoubtedly there were other variables, both situational and psychological, at work in these patients but one fact stood out above all—drug usage was a central factor in the overall picture. Invariably marijuana was the first drug used and its use often had continued without interruption. These patients had lost their interest in life or, if not all of their interest, their ability to masterfully adapt. Slowly but surely they had sunk in their social adjustment. Many described how their anxieties about life were calmed by marijuana and how after a while nothing seemed to matter any more. In some patients it seemed as if the use of marijuana initiated the regressive, disintegrative process: in other patients other factors had induced the regression and marijuana smoking began later. But in all patients it seemed absolutely clear to me that the substance became a powerful factor in the continuation of the patient's downhill course.

Treatment was *always* made more difficult when marijuana smoking continued. Just as in life generally, the patients who continued to use marijuana were difficult to reach; they were more refractory to constructive therapeutic intervention. They lacked the motivation to change, to get back into the mainstream of life; they were willing to settle for less and many seemed willing to settle for nothing at all except a place to sleep, eat, and regress. Despite the staff's best efforts to isolate them from the drug, many managed to continue to use it. For inpatient psychiatric treatment to be effective, cessation of the use of marijuana was essential.

The most shocking and heartbreaking observations are those I have made on the changes of young people I have known personally for a long period of time. The typical picture is that of a young person full of vitality, socially involved, and steadily climbing in his advance through life. Most were in high school or college, goal-directed, and making their grades. Then because of inner need or because of peer pressure, these lively young people began smoking marijuana. Slowly but surely their personalities began to change and their life adjustments deteriorated. Their appearances changed. One boy in particular looked grotesque. Another brilliant young man has been unable to even come close to realizing his potential.

In order to expand the data base of non-patient young people, my two sons, one a medical student (now a physician) and the other an undergraduate (now a graduate student), participated in the observation and assessment of behavior with regard to the effects of marijuana on their peers. The physician son stated: "With chronic usage the effects are lack of motivation, lack of direction, inability to concentrate, lack of tenacity, and difficulty directing attention.... The effects are generally not recognized by the user.... Personality changes are slow and insidious.... There is a deterioration in appearance, hostility toward authority, a trend toward uncooperativeness.... A way of life is established characterized by choice of music, friends, mannerisms, cliques. It is very hard for the individual to break away from the close-knit group of marijuana smokers, which seeks to enlist new members. Chronic use for years hooks the person into a lifestyle which is extremely hard to break."

My graduate-student son stated: "What I observed is a lack of drive and a washing out of the person's emotions. There is a loss of respect for so-called straight people and a general lack of caring for others. They deteriorate in about six months, don't realize it and have to be off the drug for several months before they clear up. Lack of goal directedness is the main effect on the older user. All users seem to live in a different kind of reality." Very few stop using the drug.

As a cross check on these observations, I interviewed several high school teachers. The questions were simple and straightforward: "Can you tell when one of your students is smoking marijuana, and will you describe its effects?" The teachers' initial response was one of surprise and disbelief that there might be any doubt about their answer. All responded affirmatively, that they could tell. Students who smoked marijuana typically became less attentive, they lost their motivation to learn and participate meaningfully in class, their performance began to slip, and some eventually dropped out of school altogether. Usually their appearance would change for the worse; hair got longer, they were less neat, and the "far out" clothing styles appeared in some. Overall they were more alienated from the teacher. These observers spontaneously would embellish their comments by giving a few examples of a bright, involved young person who eventually became completely lost. Comments were: "It was tragic to see this happen, but what could I do, etc., etc. Someone should have intervened." These teachers had made discreet inquiries about what these students were doing. The answer was that so-and-so is on marijuana.

Most of my psychiatrist colleagues believe chronic use of marijuana is harmful. Those who smoke marijuana tend to believe the substance is harmless. These men have both inpatient and outpatient practice. They qualify their remarks by saying the basic ego strength of the individual, the quantity of the drug taken, and other factors determine the effects. They agreed, however, that the psychological effects range from minor to very harmful.

I should mention here that I have spoken on the effects of marijuana dozens of times to very large audiences, on radio and on local and national television. After each such appearance I have been deluged by letters and phone calls from parents who report that what I described as regards the effects of marijuana is precisely what happened to their son or daughter. Former drug users report the same facts and many have stated that they are not the same people they used to be despite having been off marijuana for many months or years. A few persons call who are using drugs, pleading for help. There are always those drug users who approach me after a public appearance who loudly proclaim the harmlessness of drugs. Their appearance is usually shabby; it is impossible to know what station in life they might be occupying if they had never gotten on drugs. From my experience, I believe most of them would be substantially further along in their level of achievement.

More direct in-depth observation on the effects of marijuana were possible through the psychoanalytic treatment of young adults who continued to use the drug during treatment. In addition to providing longitudinal observations, it is now clear that it is a mistake to try to do psychotherapy for the substance-abuser, including those who use marijuana. Several observations merit reporting. Without any question marijuana has the effect of impairing the patient's motivation for achieving constructive change. At times, with the exercise of much willpower and bolstered by encouragement from the doctor, patients would abstain for varying periods of time. Improved alertness, greater motivation for treatment and for improving life generally was the inevitable result. However, this very improvement also generated adaptational anxiety which was caused by the mobilization of unconscious conflicts. Ideally the therapeutic process exposes these mobilized unconscious conflicts and, if treatment goes well, they are resolved and the patient is relieved of his neurotic conflicting burdens. The marijuana smoker, however, like the alcoholic or any other drug-using individual, is very prone to resume smoking and regress rather than face his inner conflicts, resolve them, and mature.

In several patients the unconscious meaning attached to the mental state associated with marijuana smoking was especially clear. Rather than face life and master it, the anxiety and the prior use of marijuana opens up the regressive route to the blissful state similar to that of an infant who has just been satiated by having been nursed and cared for by his mother. The few patients I have successfully treated who were smoking marijuana were not heavy users and there were environmental resources available which could be used to isolate them from the drug. My psychotherapy supervisees report essentially the same findings. In brief, the patient is typically lacking in drive to change, he is failing in his life adjustment, he is socially alienated, and so on. When the use of marijuana ceases, the eventual improvement in mental clarity and motivation is dramatic.

Florid psychosis occurred in two of my patients. In one, the patient's psychosis lasted six months. In the other, acute panic and paranoid ideation cleared within twelve hours.

The requisite steps for curing the chronic marijuana user, both inpatient and outpatient, in whom personality change has occurred, provide further evidence of the depth of the effects of the drug. Reason alone, which focuses on obvious personality and life adjustment effects, even those acknowledged by the user, rarely produces positive results. Nor will insight into the unconscious conflictual factors which led to the use of marijuana bring about positive change. This latter point became completely clear to me after using what seemed to be very skillful and precise insight with my patients, only to find that positive responses to insight were fleeting at best. Occasionally a patient would abstain for a week or two but eventually the urge to smoke, often combined with overt or subtle pressure from friends, prevailed and the patient lapsed into his old pattern.

In my experience there is only one certain way to be cured from marijuana smoking. The user must be totally isolated from the drug for a minimum of three months. Only after a period of sustained abstinence will the user become aware of the profound effects the drug has had on him and at the same time become free of its addictive effects. The inability of the user to perceive himself or gain insight into what has happened to him over time is one of the truly pernicious and remarkable aspects of the effects of marijuana. Talking rarely works; forthright decisive action by someone willing and able to take responsibility for the fate of the user is necessary. The chronic and heavy and, probably even moderate user, cannot take responsibility for himself. If no message other than this one is registered by the reader my effort will be justified many times over. How the person or persons exercise their responsibility to the user depends on the age of the user, his life circumstances, the severity of the retrogressive changes, and the deterioration of the user. I recommend sparing no effort whatsoever in assuming responsibility. Someone who cares must intervene, totally, consistently, and with unrelenting perseverance. *Never* give up until you have won the battle. Efforts short of an all-out effort generally fail.

In summary, I believe chronic marijuana use affects memory, judgment, motivation, perception, cognition, and affect. In addition, the drug causes an overall deterioration of personality; it leads to an estrangement from the mainstream of life; it lowers performance in all areas; and it leads to a social phenomenon in which users bond together into both loose and tightly bound subsocial groups. The effects on the user's family life are frequently devastating.

SOME BASIC FACTS ABOUT MARIJUANA AND OTHER DRUGS

The most commonly used drug, after alcohol, is marijuana. Much false information about marijuana is circulated by people who profit from the sale of this substance. Marijuana generates 25 to 35 billion dollars of profit every year. More money is made in California growing marijuana than grapes! The pro-marijuana crowd is very large and very powerful, but slowly the truth about this substance is coming to light despite their influence on the communications media.

The marijuana now being sold is anywhere from five to ten times stronger than before. Some of the earlier research studies were based on the older, less potent varieties; many of those studies were not carefully done, and quite understandably negative results frequently turned up. More recently, the findings are showing that marijuana is harmful. This development is similar in some ways to the way the truth finally surfaced as regards the harmful effects of cigarette smoking. The American Medical Association has stated marijuana is a harmful substance.

One of the most important facts to know about marijuana is that there are about 400 different chemicals in the smoke, of which there are several active chemicals in addition to THC (the most active chemical), that cause the effects desired by the user. Unlike alcohol which is used up in about twenty-four hours or less, the active ingredients of marijuana remain in the body for about thirty days. When a joint of marijuana is smoked, about one-half of the active ingredients are still in the body seven days later. You can easily see that a joint per week or even every other week keeps the body tissues under the influence of the active chemicals constantly. Marijuana seeks out tissues of the body which are high in fat content. The brain and testicles and ovaries are the parts of the body which absorb most of the active ingredients of marijuana. Someone who smokes marijuana daily or every other day is continuously intoxicated even though the "high" which follows immediately after inhaling marijuana smoke has subsided.

Obviously then, the old saying, "It doesn't matter what you do while not at work, just don't do it while at work," does not apply to marijuana. When you smoke marijuana after working hours, you bring the long-range effects of marijuana to work with you. This will become clearer to you when the long-range effects of marijuana are described.[24]

I. THE IMMEDIATE EFFECTS OF MARIJUANA:

The "high" which is the result of inhaling marijuana smoke lasts for an hour or two on to several hours, depending on the potency of the marijuana and how much is smoked and on individual differences in the susceptibility to the substance.

So-called psychomotor functions become impaired to some extent during this "high." Coordination, attention, concentration, memory, orientation to time and space are all impaired. The likelihood of causing an accident or making a mistake are increased during a "high." You are more likely to hurt or kill yourself along with your work associates if you are "high" on duty. It is irresponsible, self-destructive, and destructive to others to interfere in any way with your ability to do your job well by coming to work stoned (high on marijuana) or under the influence of any other drug, including alcohol.

II. LONG-RANGE EFFECTS OF MARIJUANA:

A. *The Brain*: Some research studies have reported no evidence that the brain shrinks after prolonged marijuana use. You should know that millions of brain cells would have to be destroyed before visual tests of brain shrinkage such as the X-ray or CT Scan would be positive. However, when the brain cells of monkeys which have received moderate to heavy exposure to marijuana are examined by means of the electron microscope which magnifies the cells many thousands of times, severe changes are observable.[25] The interior of the brain cell is markedly altered and the space between the cells which transmits the signals between cells is widened and thickened. Furthermore, electrical tracings from the deeper regions of the brain show abnormal electrical discharges. Abnormal electrical brain waves from the surface of the brains of young people who were smoking marijuana have been reported.

B. *Changes in Personality and Behavior*: The brain cell changes which were described in the preceding paragraph are entirely consistent with the long-term effects of marijuana use on personality, behavior, and psychological functions. One doctor referred to the personality changes as early senility. Marijuana smokers eventually lose their drive, their motivation. The achievement of high goals loses its importance. Performance inevitably falls off. Marijuana smokers rarely achieve higher levels of success, and most unfortunately lose the ground they have gained. Memory begins to go bad, especially for recent events. The ability to think is impaired. This is especially so when the task involves reasoning, logic, and abstract thinking. Emotions eventually wash out.

Pot smokers in time become colorless and emotionally flat. Some become suspicious and tend to believe others have evil intentions toward them. Marijuana smokers are apt to withdraw from their families and from the organizations to which they belong. They become absorbed into themselves and care very little about others. They tend to see authority as bad rather than as friendly or kind leadership. There is an overall deterioration in their personality. Their appearance and their living spaces are less neat.

Some marijuana smokers become severely mentally ill with one of the major mental illnesses. There have been cases reported where the person becomes insane after very little exposure to marijuana.

Very young people who smoke marijuana tend not to mature as well as they should. This finding may be related to the fact that pot smokers eventually become very passive. Normal male aggressiveness is lost.

C. *Effects on Reproduction, Testicles, Ovaries, and Hormones*: The sperm of pot smoking males loses its vigor. There are more abnormal forms. In mice, the production of sperm can be completely wiped out. Fortunately, these changes return to normal when marijuana has not been used for several months.

Several investigators have reported a lowering in humans and experimental animals of the male hormone, testosterone. To be a normal young man, you need a normal amount of testosterone. It has been reported that the blood levels of testosterone are increased in pot-smoking females.

About 10% of the pregnancies of the monkey are normally lost. In monkeys exposed to marijuana at the level defined as moderate to heavy use in humans, the number of incomplete pregnancies jumps to over 40%. Hormone changes occur in the female too, and it is probable that these changes account for these incomplete pregnancies. Marijuana disturbs the menstrual cycle in women.

The offspring of experimental animals exposed to marijuana while pregnant have normal babies. However, when the males reach puberty their total body weight is less and their testicles are smaller than the offspring of mothers who were not exposed to marijuana when they were pregnant.

D. *The Immune System*: The boy's immune system is impaired to some degree. The white blood cells which fight infection show changes; they lose their capacity to divide and thereby increase their number. Pot smokers are more susceptible to infections, and it is probable that these white cell changes are the reason.

E. *Chromosomes*: Several researchers have reported changes in the chromosomes. Chromosomes are that part of the cell which governs the formation of the body as it is developing and much more. Much of the mystery of life is hidden in the chromosomes.

F. *The Lungs*: Marijuana smoke contains approximately 50% more irritating and potentially cancer-producing chemicals than tobacco smoke. Studies of the cells lining the airways show severe irritation, and some have reported pre-cancerous changes as a consequence of exposure to marijuana smoke. Degenerative changes have been reported in experimental animals exposed to marijuana smoke. It has been noted that experimental animals die of lung infections more frequently after exposure to marijuana smoke.

Marijuana is a health and life-destroying substance. It is *not* one of the so-called soft drugs. You can get hooked on it, and it will get to you eventually. Marijuana will not kill you suddenly as happens when a person overdoses on certain drugs. Death does not always come suddenly; it can creep up on you slowly and parts of you die slowly. Marijuana will eventually damage and even destroy your mind and your ability to function effectively in life if you smoke it heavily enough. Sometimes these changes come slowly and sometimes they come rapidly, but they come. The "burn out" condition is very real. What you have read is not meant to be a "scare tactic."

Some marijuana smokers protest loudly that they are getting along in life. There is no way for them to know what height of achievement they might have attained had they not smoked pot. Many of these protesters look rather seedy, but of course they cannot see themselves. Marijuana users usually cannot recognize the changes which are occurring within themselves until a month, or usually several months, has passed after stopping marijuana use. Then they look back and can see how severely their behavior was altered.

You cannot be a fully effective person if you smoke marijuana. You will also be increasing the possibility of making a mistake which will injure or kill yourself and others too. Sooner or later marijuana will do its damage in one or in many different ways.

Marijuana frequently leads to other drugs. Tolerance builds up to marijuana as the brain tissue becomes nonresponsive or is destroyed. Greater quantities are used. Some people then turn to other drugs.

If you stop smoking marijuana soon enough, chances are you will bounce back and become once again what you once were. Not always. Some never get it all back. Even they recognize they have "lost something." The heavier smokers lose out in life. Others have progressed while they fell by the wayside. The pot smoker sees this especially clearly after he has been off of marijuana for sixty days or more.

Then the discouragement and depression set in when he sees how far he has fallen behind.

III. **LSD:**

LSD is a very toxic substance which has a powerful effect on the mind. Severe alterations in perception, the ability to think, and motor coordinator occur. You cannot possibly do your job under the influence of this substance. Some people become seriously mentally ill after using LSD, and they do not always respond to medication. Some remain hospitalized for a very long time. So-called "flash backs" develop in some people long after they have stopped using LSD.

IV. **COCAINE:**

Cocaine causes a relatively brief "rush" or "high." People get hooked on cocaine too and get so desperate for it they inject it in their veins every few hours. Cocaine can destroy you too. The cost of maintaining the cocaine habit is very great, and the result can be that you will carry out criminal acts to finance your habit.

V. **HEROIN:**

Heroin is a substance that causes severe addiction. Heroin addiction is a very serious condition which will eventually disable you. You cannot remain an effective and productive individual if you use heroin. Do not try it; people get hooked very quickly. Many heroin addicts started on marijuana, and when they no longer could get high on it, they turned to other drugs, frequently heroin.

VI. ALCOHOL:

Now a few comments about alcohol are in order. Moderate alcohol consumption will not destroy you. Millions of people consume alcohol with moderation and get along very well in life. However, excessive use of alcohol is obviously very bad. Many fatal accidents have been caused by drunkenness. Heavy use of alcohol does eventually damage the brain and other organs in the body.

VII. UPPERS AND DOWNERS:

Amphetamine and similar substances as well as sedatives of various kinds and tranquilizers all alter behavior. People get hooked on these drugs too. Some go on to other drugs as their tolerance builds up. If you think you need a stimulant or sedative, go to a doctor and find out what is the matter with you.

Many young people say, "You have your alcohol, and we have marijuana." The comparison is full of error, and two wrongs do not make a right. Remember, alcohol is used up in the body at about the rate of an ounce per hour. One-half of the active chemicals in marijuana are still in the body seven days later, and traces remain for as long as thirty days. Regular use of marijuana leads to a build-up of the active chemicals in the body.

VIII. PCP

PCP is an extremely dangerous chemical which can produce very violent behavior and severe mental damage. This chemical is probably the most damaging of all of the so-called street drugs.

IX: SUMMING UP:

Take very seriously what you have just read. Do not risk injuring or killing yourself and others through an accident because of drugs. Do not throw away the precious gift of life by losing vital qualities or functions of your personality through the slow, partial death which marijuana and other drugs cause.

If you cannot kick the drug habit alone, then turn to someone for help. Ask your friends or family to ride through the storms of drug withdrawal with you. If that doesn't work, turn yourself in for professional help.

A final word to you non-drug users. Take the initiative and try very hard to get your friends and family members off drugs. They have been wounded by chemicals. You would save an injured friend or family member, then save your friends and family members and work associates from drugs. Be your brother's keeper. At first, they may resent your intervention; but when you have helped them turn the tide, they will love you for having helped them. It is in their best interest and in the best interest of America for everyone to be off drugs. Can you think of a higher calling than to help someone get off drugs and possibly even save someone from slow or sudden death?

In my opinion, the influx of illegal drugs into the United States constitutes a national crisis and should be combated by the use of any and all methods until the use of these substances has been completely stopped. An all-out effort seems essential to me, in view of the enormous harm being done to millions of Americans and to our society. Current law enforcement efforts and community educational programs, while helpful, will never be adequate. Far too many children and young people do not live in intact families. Too many parents are either indifferent to the problem, or they are too frightened to take the necessary steps to protect their children. Some families simply cannot provide a barrier between drugs and their children because of their living circumstances, social pressures, and work demands. Teachers cannot possibly take on this task. Drug users usually laugh at educational materials. Local law enforcement agencies are swamped by other law-enforcing responsibilities including the arrest of the big drug pushers. What then can be done?

The drug epidemic must be attacked from two directions. The demand for drugs must be dried up, and those who supply drugs must be stopped cold in their tracks.

ELIMINATING THE DEMAND FOR DRUGS

The *first step* in eliminating the demand for drugs is educational. This process is underway but a massive effort should be launched to bring the facts to the public. The pro-drug lobby is very powerful. The facts, particularly about the harmful effects of marijuana, have been suppressed by elements within the communications media and much misinformation has been disseminated. Those who want to limit or reduce legal restrictions on the use of drugs, especially marijuana, are a powerful force in our society and they spare no effort to discredit those of us who have carried messages regarding the harmfulness of drugs to the public.

The purpose of education is to provide the basis for individuals to take responsibility for themselves and to cease using drugs, or never start using drugs in the first place. Education also provides the basis for responsible people to take responsibility for those who will not or who cannot take responsibility for themselves.

The *second step* is for the non-user of drugs to help the users quit using drugs. Such a strategy may sound odd or unworkable, but I believe the plan will work, and here is why.

Recently the prevalence of drug abuse in the Navy and Marine Corps in the younger members of these two services was approximately 47%. In order to address this grave problem, these services launched a massive campaign designed to bring the facts to "all hands." Dogs for detection and urine analyzers are used to detect users. When caught, users are faced with punishment. Officers and chief petty officers are immediately discharged from the service. Younger service men and women are offered treatment. They may be punished, but they are given a second chance. The second element, therefore, in the program is the shadow of threat. Incidentally *any* drug user may ask for treatment; he will receive it, and his service record will be damaged in no way at all.

Education and threat will make a substantial dent in the problem, but a large number of substance abusers will not respond; they will deny (to themselves) the harmful effects of drugs, or they will believe they can escape detection and punishment.

My main contribution to the Navy and Marine Corps war on drugs was the proposal that the non-users of drugs be inspired by Naval and Marine leadership to work upon their shipmates and friends who use drugs and get them to quit. The concept is called peer responsibility/pressure. It amounts to being one's brother's keeper or the stronger taking responsibility for the weaker. The willingness to take this responsibility is based upon the inherent altruism which exists in us all—that willingness to extend a helping hand to a fellow human in trouble. Where non-users of drugs and drug-users work closely together, the desire to help a drug-user is also based on the instinct of self-preservation. Drug-users are more likely to make a mistake and cause an accident. Therefore, on the risk factor alone, it is to everyone's advantage to not have one's functioning impaired by chemicals.

The power bases upon which the peer responsibility concept will work are the bonds of friendship and the common bond of organizational identity. If you *really care* about another person, you don't stand by and watch him destroy himself; you intervene. Furthermore, you don't stand by and let him influence your own life negatively or even destroy it. Drugs eventually destroy everyone just as surely as a bullet.

In fact, this is an analogy I made to the leaders of the Navy and Marine Corps. I pointed out that men in battle rescue their wounded even at the expense of someone's life. Drug-users are often as badly wounded as men in the battlefield; someone must save them. It is up to us non-users of drugs to do so. This program was phenomenally successful.

Within nine months or so the level of drug use in the Navy among sailors in the first five enlisted grades dropped from 47% to 21.8%! The extent to which the peer responsibility/pressure strategy contributed to this dramatic decline is hard to know, but much credit is given to this approach.

How then to apply the peer responsibility/pressure strategy to society at large? Our society is made up of all kinds of organizations. All organizations have managerial leadership just as the Navy and Marine Corps have their leadership. The message should be sent to the leadership of *every organization* in our society that it has become their added responsibility to inspire the members of their organizations to quit using drugs, and, *in particular,* inspire the non-users of drugs to help those who use drugs to quit. The President of the United States, I believe, should deliver his inspirational guidance to the public.

The method worked, and is working in the Navy and Marine Corps. The Chief of Naval Operations and the Commandant of the Marine Corps delivered the message. Naval and Marine Corps leadership and vast numbers of non-users of drugs responded. I believe our President could inspire many of the leaders of our societies' organizations, who in turn could continuously activate the peer responsibility/pressure strategy within their own organizations.

The *third step* is for parents to take responsibility for their children. The strategy for combating drug use within the family has been described in my booklet, *How To Get Your Child Off Marijuana.*[26] The essentials are for the parents to first determine whether or not their child is using drugs. Next, tell the drug-using child he must stop and provide the facts which will legitimize the parents' demand. These steps may suffice in some families, but for many, these relatively mild interventions will not work at all. The key is to separate the child from drugs, no matter what steps have to be taken to bring this about. Substitute family time for the drugs. Help the child find new goals, and often, new friends.

Because of the addictive effects of drugs and the psychological regression associated with drug usage, and because of the long time (up to forty-five days) it takes the body to cleanse itself of marijuana, improvement in the drug-user's mental condition will not appear immediately. Improvement will come eventually. Work hard at saving your children; no one else will do it for you. If you do not, the probability of tragedy is great, and should tragedy strike, you will never get over it completely; your guilt will dog you for the rest of your life. If ever there was a situation where the parent must be his child's keeper, it is when the child gets hooked on drugs.

ELIMINATING THE SUPPLY OF DRUGS

The ultimate and only effective method for winning the war on drugs is to make it impossible for people to get drugs. I believe a substantial reduction in demand can be achieved, but there will always be some children whose parents will not intervene, or who do not have parents. There are many adults who will escape, or not respond to the peer responsibility/pressure strategy, and will refuse to believe the facts about drugs. Most of these poor souls are psychologically vulnerable people who turned to drugs and cannot get off.

Just as a good strong father must protect his family from hostile and destructive influences so too must our government protect our society from drugs. Our nation is under attack by chemicals just as dangerously as if a hostile nation were attacking us in the classic military sense. We are at war. Our government must counterattack and I predict our armed forces will one day be used in an all-out effort to win this war. Currently our military forces are used for detection, but these efforts are woefully inadequate. The importation of drugs into our country, and the growing and manufacture of drugs within our borders must be completely eliminated. Very harsh measures will ultimately have to be used. I advocate use of such measures and given a committed President, I predict such measures will eventually be employed. If ever there was a time for a Call to Arms to win a well-defined war, it is *now*. Mr. President, as Commander-in-Chief, the time has come for you to unleash our military so they can destroy the enemy (drugs) which is destroying millions of our fellow-Americans. Mr. President, the time has come for you to inspire the non-users of drugs to save those who have been wounded by drugs—as men do in the field of battle.

Chapter XI

Parenting

It is not my intent to discuss all of the ramifications of parenting. Many volumes would be required to thoroughly discuss the subject. It would be necessary to describe the effects of the parent's personality on the child, the nature of the developmental process in children (and in parents), how the mind works, and a myriad of other aspects of this broad subject. I wish only to focus on a few aspects of parental responsibility, in particular on parental authority and certain basic values. Authority has become a bad word in modern-day society and evidence exists everywhere that authority is breaking down in our society and in the home. This trend is a major element in the weakening of our society.

A moment's reflection will soon lead to the conclusion that "authority" really is nothing more than a set of rules or guidelines for living. Rules, laws, traditions, values are nothing more than structures which channel the human spirit and govern conduct so that people get along reasonably well with each other, do minimal harm to themselves, and to others, and live constructively. Behind the laws there exists the threat of punishment if one deviates too far.

Ideally people should live by laws, customs, etc.

because they possess within themselves sufficient authority to do so and possess an adequate capacity for reasoned thought so as to be able to comprehend the consequences when we do or do not live by the rules. Truly mature people live by the rules of civilized society because they have sufficient inner authority to do so; they do not need the police, or a threat of punishment to force them to live by the rules of society.

Not only are the rules of society breaking down, but the capacity of people to live by the rules is weakening. These facts can be traced directly to the breakdown of authority within the home, *and* to the revolutionary changes which are taking place in society's values. Parenting is extremely difficult these days. Young people in increasing numbers defy parental authority and they are disregarding time-tested values, traditions, codes of conduct on a massive scale. Those parents who can successfully uphold the solid values and continue to serve as loved authorities for their children are becoming a rarity.

Parents, I *urge* you not to abandon those time-tested principles that most of us learned from our own parents, in school and in church. Remember change does not always mean progress. Life *is* ever-changing, to be sure, but change has to be studied carefully and tested before it is possible to know if the direction of change is progressive or not. Generally, changes which evolve slowly are more constructive than sudden, revolutionary changes. The revolutionary redefinition of what constitutes a family is the most alarming example I can think of. The family is the oldest and most stable organizational pattern of civilized (and pre-civilized) man, yet within a few years the word "family" has been re-defined to mean almost anything.

Parents are losing faith in themselves and in the institutions which have traditionally been the guardians of our values, namely, the Church and the university. Almost any life style can be found on or around a university campus, and its advocate within the classrooms. The churches have lost less ground, but even there certain basic human values and truths are being questioned. What then shall parents believe? And what shall they uphold to their children?

Parents, believe what *you* believe; chances are you will be closer to rationality—the truth—than the avant garde protagonists of the wave of the future. Think about your beliefs, about concepts like honesty, integrity, morality, commitment, duty, honor, responsibility, fidelity, etc.—re-read the Ten Commandments! Then decide who, after all, is on the right track, you or some advocate of social change (teacher, minister, or whomever). Stick by your guns and live by your beliefs *and expect your children to do the same.* They are your children, not society's. It is *your* responsibility to help them grow into mature, responsible adults. Most elements in society could not care less about what happens to your children. Of course, there still are good teachers and ministers, but keep an ever-vigilant eye on who is influencing your child.

Advocating certain values to your children and expecting them to live by them is the first step. The second step is the more difficult one—getting them to follow your lead, to live by what you taught them. Here is where parental authority enters the picture. Children abide by parental authority for essentially two reasons: (1) out of love and respect for the parent and (2) out of fear, fear of rejection or punishment.

Parents who have had a good relationship with their child will have much greater success in having their children follow their guidelines on the basis of love and respect. Ideally the element of fear should never have to be resorted to by the parent. Inevitably children test parental guidelines and authority. The art of parenting is to be able to know when to let children test new ways, and how far to let them go, and when not to and when to draw the line.

In general, parental authority has deteriorated badly in our society. No clearer evidence of this exists than the push to make it possible for minor children to sue their parents. No one endorses parental abuse of children, and no effort should be spared to protect children from physical and psychological abuse. However, when parental authority is destroyed, the child is *also* abused. Those who have not internalized parental authority are unable to live by society's authority.

It is imperative, therefore, not only for the sake of the child's personality development, but also for the stability and growth of society that parents again exercise benevolent authority with their children. I cannot possibly describe in detail how far parents should go in the exercise of authority. The principle, however, is a clear one. Set the ground rules for living and expect them to be followed. Parents should be consistent and always try to present a unified position to the children. Do not let the children play one parent against the other. Have no hesitation in using the phrase "I say so" in response to your child's defiant "Who says so?" Do not fear a clash with your children. Life cannot be lived without confrontation.

Parents should listen to the child's point of view and if the child is right, then change course and go his way. But if not, then hold firm, and if a confrontation develops, do not be afraid of it. I have seen some extremely intense confrontations between parent and offspring. Emotions ran high, but eventually the child recognized that the parent was right. Almost without exception a better relationship developed between parent and child subsequent to the confrontation.

No more compelling issues exists than drug use and swinging sexual behavior by young people. If you intervene and stand on an unshakeable barrier between your child and drugs, the child will one day recognize how much you really loved, and love him and will be forever grateful. Do not think you will win your child's love and respect by being tolerant of his drug use. You will almost surely lose your child and his respect for you as well. You are fooling yourself if you think you are winning your child's respect by adopting his freewheeling ways of living and dressing. The tension between you and the child will diminish or disappear but so will his admiration and respect for you.

Remember President Truman's low popularity with the public when he stood firm on certain national and international issues. Now most people respect him deeply for being strong enough to take a stand and make good the phrase—"The buck stops here." Your popularity with your child may temporarily drop quite low, but later it will be very high. You will be promoting personality growth in your children, building their character by being a loving authority.

In this chapter I have not described the intricacies of the developmental processes which occur from birth to death. How the personalities of the parents, family life, and other factors foster personality development is a fascinating subject and can be understood by a person of average intelligence. Some knowledge of this topic can be very helpful to individuals in working out a successful life adjustment, in particular when that adjustment includes the responsibilities of marriage and parenthood.

The companion piece to this volume, discusses the main principles of childhood development, explains why people fail and become psychologically ill, and offers some guidelines for improving one's personal life.

Chapter XII

Can America Survive? A Call to Arms

The vitality of a nation is the sum of the vitality of its people. The vitality of a nation is reflected in its productive efficiency, its creativeness in all aspects of life, ranging across the spectrum from the sciences to the humanities and the arts. A nation's vitality is also reflected in its values, traditions, laws, and social mores. America has ranked at the top in nearly all aspects of this definition of a vital nation. The free world has relied upon us for leadership and protection.

In order for individual vitality to be able to contribute to national vitality each individual must have the freedom to develop his potential and express it in the society which creates him. Too rigid a social structure enslaves the human spirit and fails to evoke and develop human potential. Tradition stabilizes a society but societies that are too tradition-bound do not keep pace with the social progress enjoyed by freer societies.

In America we have produced very vital and strong individuals. These individuals have been able to find the opportunities to express their abilities, and as a consequence ours has been a very vigorous nation. We enjoy enormous freedom, and our society permits social change to occur. It is imperative that social change be constructive. While the United States is still the source of strength for the stability of the world, serious doubt is being expressed by many thoughtful individuals within our own nation, and from nations whose security depends on us, whether we possess the national will to carry on in this leadership and protective capacity. Our pre-eminence is slipping away clearly and unmistakably. The Soviet Union is not only arming at a furious rate, the Soviets are beginning to flaunt their power under our noses. Cuba, with Soviet backing, is taking liberties in Africa which it dared not do fifteen to twenty years ago. Now and then one reads an editorial written by sober, experienced observers of the international scene who express some doubt if we could win the next war.

The United States Treasury, at one time, seemed inexhaustible. We have financed the rebuilding of the nations we destroyed in war. We have sponsored the growth of underdeveloped nations. Our national debt has grown steadily as those in charge lacked the vision or courage and strength required to place restraint on policies which created the huge national debt. For the first time in history, our government no longer borrows just from its own people, but is borrowing money from foreign countries as well. This trend reflects a serious weakness in the leadership of America and in the national will.

Equally ominous is the lowered productive efficiency of the United States. The reproductive efficiency of the other industrialized nations is increasing while ours is decreasing. The United States is now ranked the lowest in productive efficiency among the industrialized nations of the West. Great worry exists among our national leaders about our lag in technological innovation.

While the balance of trade deficit is in part attributable to oil imports, this factor by no means accounts for all of the deficit. Japan has no oil whatsoever yet has a huge trade surplus. Their productive efficiency is increasing while ours is dropping. Their people work harder and more efficiently. The family unit is very solid in Japan, perhaps as strong as anywhere else in the world.

Predictably the value of the dollar has dropped at home and abroad despite its recent strength brought about by high interest rates. This decline in part reflects the opinion other nations have of the American character and its will. Our leaders have debased the dollar. Leaders of iron will who can manage finances wisely, who do not overspend, no longer seem to exist. No leader seems to exist who has the courage to say *No* to the insatiable demands of virtually every sector of society. Instead, the printing press rolls on and on, and inflation will spiral ever upward despite a temporary decline.

While high interest rates have temporarily strengthened the dollar, the consequences are high unemployment and serious recession, if not outright depression. It is but a matter of time before the weakened will of our leaders manifests itself and we reinflate again. Federal deficits have *never* permanently diminished. What is happening to America?

The answer to that question is not difficult to find. *Americans* have changed and are continuing to change.[27] As they change, social values change. Currently the direction of that change is toward disintegration and weakness rather than strength. The present day leadership of America was put there by a changed people. The key question is whether a sufficient number of strong Americans exist so as to be able to outvote the weak Americans who have placed weak leaders in power. A strong president can be completely crippled by a Congress which gives in to the will of the people who want to *get* from their country rather than *give* to it.

In view of the fact that the divorce rate continues to climb—it is now 50%—and that approximately one-half of our young people are spending a major portion of their developmental years in living arrangements other than true families, our future is uncertain at best. This is so because all of those personality factors, the confluence of which lead to strength of character, strength of will, capacity for commitment, the ability to work hard, the quest for excellence will be diminished to some degree in millions of young people whose responsibility it will be to carry our society forward.

These millions of individuals will inevitably select leaders for government who will promise to give to them rather than expect to get from them. A child who has been deprived during his early developmental years lives his life wanting to get from others; he continually attempts to fill himself up in one way or

Can America Survive? A Call to Arms 157

another. By contrast, those who have received abundant emotional input from their parents during their developmental years, are full of life and go out into the world with the capacity to give to life, and make society move forward. Multiply this formula by the millions of children who have missed out on bountiful home life, and it provides a clearer picture of why it is probable that the public will place weak leaders in office who will give them what they want and thereby ever increase the size of the national debt.

As the national debt grows, inflation will re-ignite and more women will be forced out of the home and into the work place. Their babies and small children will be more deprived than filled. When they grow up, they will trend toward wanting to *take from* rather than *contribute to* society. They will join the swelling ranks of those who elect leaders who will give them what they want, ever increasing the size of the national debt and so on and on until the currency becomes worthless, and the economy collapses. We are already well on our way. Despite our president's very sincere wish to reduce the size of the federal debt, he is failing. The voice of those who want nurture is too loud. Granted there are truly needy people and the governmental steps to reverse inflation have caused many to become unemployed through no weakness of character of their own, yet there are too many in government who lack the strength of character to stand firm and correct the economic ills.

Other nations always know when a nation is becoming weak. The international scene is a dog-eat-dog world; nations always exist which will quickly fill a vacuum. The Soviet Union is demonstrating this principle most clearly at present. If America becomes weak, it is absolutely predictable that revolutions will occur in smaller countries and they will promptly fall within the Soviet sphere of influence. When the balance of power is sufficiently great against us and our Western allies, the Soviets will unquestionably make a major move.

America is a compassionate nation, but the massive immigration into our country is cause for deep concern. The flagrant way Castro dumped his "undesirables" on us was successful because our administration was too weak to prevent this shocking event from occurring. People made the decision to let them in. Look at their strength of character, and you will see weakness and passivity behind the facade of compassion. Rome was eventually invaded, and so are we being invaded because we have become too weak to erect and enforce immigration barriers.

Many who do immigrate will undoubtedly embrace the solid values of America and contribute to her strength, but vast numbers will not. There has not been sufficient time for them to thoroughly accommodate to our values. Generally the strongest supporters of any nation's values are those who are born in that nation, grew up in a solid family, and adapted to that nation's values from childhood onward.

This is no time to "hope for the best," to assume that our situation will somehow turn itself around. We—all of us—have the responsibility to turn it around. I believe each of us has a dual responsibility. First we must try to develop our own potential to the fullest and thereby become able to make our contributions to life. Secondly, we must take a greater interest in our nation and try to save it. Each person will find his own way to do that; however, I have a few suggestions toward these objectives. We simply *must* take care of our beloved America.

Do not marry until you feel ready for it, and after you do marry, spare no effort to make your marriage succeed. A successful marriage will do more for you personally, for your children *and* for society than anything I can think of. As I have said repeatedly, the family—the healthy family—is the building block of any society; main key to civilization; it is the pivotal point around which all else turns. I urge you *not* to consider divorce until you have exhausted every possible means for making a success of your marriage. I know very well that some marriages should never have occurred. Perhaps it is just as well to dissolve them early, before children are born. However, do not assume the worst about your marriage. Many couples survive the inevitable rough waters of the early days of marriage and both parties grow emotionally as they work out their marital difficulties. It is always easier to run away from a problem than to persist and eventually solve it. The latter course nearly always brings greater rewards.

When marital strife begins, the grass always looks greener elsewhere, but it frequently is not. Give yourselves time to mature and resolve your problems. The trauma of divorce, to yourselves and to your children, is great. Spare no effort to make your marriage work.

Look squarely at how you live your personal life.

160   *Families*

Do the values you live by help or hurt you and our society? It is every person's responsibility to treat well the great gift of life. Not only will you be doing yourself a service, but you will be serving your country in this way. The writer of the Ten Commandments understood life; live by those principles. They have been tested by time and experience; live by them. In other words, re-examine the ethical system you live by and strengthen the weak spots.

Examine the social scene, and in particular, that of which you are a part. Ask yourself, "What can I do for my country that I am not now doing?" There is plenty you can do, and we had better take better care of our country, or we will lose her, if not now, almost certainly for our children and future generations. Align yourself with a social cause that interests you, but before you do, check it out very carefully, and be certain its net effect is a constructive one.

Organizations of all kinds exist and are springing up continually which are sponsored by citizen groups. Look into these and join forces with them. There are coalitions for decency, there are anti-pornography groups, anti-drug groups, all appearing throughout the land. Parents are banding together for the purpose of examining school books for the purpose of identifying those which advocate untested new life styles for the young. Groups have formed to counteract the poisonous propaganda that "gay is good"—that is, that homosexuality is a normal life style. Use your great gift of intelligence and think about the social decay which is upon us, and find an organization that is trying to do something about it, and join up, or create one of your own.

Of particular importance are legislative watchdog groups. New social values sooner or later become social norms. Some, of course, are constructive, but many are not. Someone inevitably wants to get these values written into law, and new laws do get written; some are good and some are not. The effort to "decriminalize" the use of marijuana is an example of how social values eventually influence the laws. The Women's Liberation movement's effort to change the law with regard to permitting women to enter the combat arms of the armed forces is another. Bussing schoolchildren away from their neighborhood schools is sheer madness. While the intent behind bussing was good, the effects are disastrous. The experiment simply hasn't worked, yet this monstrous injustice to our children continues.

Just as stability in the home is necessary for child development so too is stability in the school. The family, the school, and the church all provide those human experiences which lead to strength of personality. Bussing children across town breaks up the sense of continuity that is so necessary in a child's life. Parents cannot participate as well in school functions. The child lives in two worlds; one at home and the other way off somewhere at school. The sense of involvement cannot develop in the child when he is shipped away from his "home" territory.

Furthermore, adding two hours a day to a child's school day through bussing simply lacks compassion for children. They are at greater risk; they are being unnecessarily fatigued.

It is a mistake to deprive a child of racial ethnic reinforcement. Blacks are beginning to take pride in their heritage; this is as it should be. Sending Indian children to white schools damages them. Rampant alcoholism was one of the results of the white man's interference in the Indian culture.

The money and fuel that is being wasted through bussing should be spent in upgrading those schools which are below par. Children do not breed prejudice; adults do. Leave the child alone and do not take away his experiences in his neighborhood school. Therefore, elect *only* those to public office who will end one of the greatest hoaxes of our time—bussing. I believe a candidate's stand on bussing is one of the first questions he should be asked.

VALUES CLARIFICATION

People tend to forget that Boards of Education exist to serve the people by educating their children. You parents have every right to know what is being taught your children. Therefore, I urge you to organize yourselves and check on your schools. In particular, take careful note of what is being taught in social studies, psychology, that is, in the humanities. The area of so-called "values clarification" needs to be looked into. I believe it is constructive for children to know themselves and to increase their level of awareness of social problems, but I do not think it is wise to permit teachers to delve into the values the child lives by. More than value clarification goes on in some schools. Teachers and counsellors also focus on the child's personality and life style in some schools. The focus at times turns to those qualities which have for centuries distinguished male from female. The subtle effect on these "value clarification" activities is to blur the differences between male and female.

The beliefs people live by are influenced by many sources. I believe it is crucial to the survival of a free society that no single source of influence have too great an impact on people, particularly the developing young. No single sector of society has cornered the market on what *Truth* is. Neither the state, the church, nor the educational institution should become excessively powerful in shaping the beliefs of a free people. Persons with a particular bias often gain excessive power, and through their segment of society influence the minds of the people. Hitler believed he had found *Truth* and through the state he had a powerful impact on the German people as well as the rest of the world.

The values people live by are continuously tested in the real world and tend to change slowly over time. This is as it should be. Be very wary of individuals or groups or movements, who tend to appear out of nowhere and proclaim to have found the "true" way to live life. We are being constantly bombarded with advice of this sort. Most of these people can be shrugged off, or their new ways of living will soon be shown unable to stand the test of the real world. However, "values clarification" in the schools is probably, on balance, more harmful than helpful. Parents, keep a watchful eye on those who influence your children!

Children do not possess an inherent wisdom which renders them capable of judging the values of society. Children must first develop their personalities, understand and live by time-tested values, and gain a certain amount of experience in life. *Then* they can challenge the values of the society in which they exist. Some bright and thoughtful young people will unquestionably create new and better values; that is how progress comes about.

Much of what goes on in schools under the heading of "values clarification" is a subtle process of inciting the young person to rebel against authority, regardless of its form, including parental authority. The developing child is thereby cast into a sea of uncertainty and defiance of those very influences (parents, home, school, church, time-tested values, etc.) which prepare the young for the challenges of life.

School time is much better spent acquiring solid knowledge of the real world and the acceptance of what older and wiser people have to tell them. A course in ethics wherein values such as honor, honesty, integrity, commitment, loyalty, etc. are discussed would be very worthwhile.

Teachers rank next in importance to parents in the life of a child. We must guide our young and give them the very best of what we have learned about and from life in order to prepare them for the responsibilities of adulthood. The last thing young people need is ambiguity, uncertainty, a reinforcement of rebelliousness, and the false belief that they possess inherent knowledge and judgment to be able to live successfully, especially in these difficult times.

The home life of millions of the young is severely limited if not non-existent. Like it or not, it is falling to our school teachers to provide more than knowledge to these children. A loving, compassionate, inspiring, dedicated teacher (especially if she possess a mature personality) can and usually has a profound effect on her pupils. Therefore teachers should project a belief in society's best values. This is an ideal, I know, but we should reach for it rather than go the other way—downhill—through the so-called "values clarification" exercises. Actually, this process blurs values.

TITLE IX

The spirit of Title IX of the Education Amendments of 1972 is being over-applied. This is especially evident in school athletic programs. The Code states that females shall be alotted as much equipment, sport activities as males, but it does not say the sexes should be mixed during sports activities. Many schools mix the sexes at the very age (puberty) when the child can ill afford to be overly stimulated by too close proximity of the opposite sex. The hormones and other maturational events are enough for these youngsters to deal with, without being in close physical contact during gym classes.

More relevant than that, however, is the fact that the superior athletic ability of the male is prevented from finding its fullest development when males are forced to engage in sports with females. In one school, flag football was played with mixed teams. When a boy passed the ball, it had to go to a female receiver, and so on to other absurdities. This arrangement simply did not work. Finally the women and men coaches agreed to separate the sexes, and boys played against boys, girls against girls. Common sense at last prevailed. In this same school boys *must* enroll in Home Economics and girls *must* enroll in Manual Arts. More nonsense! To make such enrollment optional would be the obvious and sensible arrangement.

These brief comments reflect a national trend toward blurring the differences between the sexes, at the very age when boys and girls should be developing the greatest clarity about their own gender. Many youngsters reach puberty psychologically disturbed, and the sense of identity (sexual) is nearly always involved to some degree. To then be thrown into an environment (the school—or society at large) which asserts there *are no differences* between male and female is the gravest possible injustice.

My plea is for society not to interfere with those magnificent qualities which distinguish boy from girl, man from woman. Let Nature have her way. As civilized people we must understand Nature's imperatives and foster their growth and development.

Those who object to the above-stated point of view counter by saying that mixing the sexes in every possible context deepens understanding and fosters a more comfortable articulation between the sexes. This argument is false. In order for a man and a woman to reach maximal heights in their interaction (love, sex, cooperation, depth of commitment, etc.) each must have the clearest possible sense of gender and self. *Then* and only then can male and female be truly intimate in the finest sense of the word. Imposing unisex values on the sexes, particulary during the crucial developmental years (especially so at age birth to six, and again at puberty) substantially impairs the capacity of the sexes to find the best possible intimacy. The true test of one's capacity for intimacy is marriage. Part of the blame for our current high divorce rate (50%) belongs to those who have imposed unisex values on the young.

The principle to be followed is this: Keep the sexes separate when performance relates to gender. Obviously in the classroom (English, math, history, etc.) mixing the sexes is sensible. However, where differences exist which are sex-related some degree of total separation of the sexes is wise. Where the sexes have been separated on the basis of social role, I believe individuals should be free to choose, but forced mixing of the sexes (as in home economics and manual arts, etc.) should not be done. Total freedom of choice may not be possible, but we should strive for it.

AFFIRMATIVE ACTION

The concept of affirmative action for minority races and for women was implemented in the work place in order to overcome past wrongs and present-day prejudices. Quotas have been set up. As always, concepts have to be tested in the real world. Not surprisingly, serious problems arise when the concept is implemented.

Perhaps the most serious and negative consequences of the affirmative action concept is that the most suitable person for a certain job may not be hired. Instead someone of a different race or a female is placed in the position. The immediate consequence is that *efficiency* drops. I think there is no question that one of the reasons the productive efficiency of the United States is lower than any of the rest of the industrialized nations is that managers and employers are forced by law (and often by quota) to hire people who are not the most suited for a particular task.

The low productive efficiency of the United States is a very serious matter that must be corrected, and soon. Our very vitality as a nation is at stake, our ability to maintain our freedom and our way of life will ultimately be threatened.

The principle to be followed is to fill every job in America with the most suitable person possible. Freedom of choice for managers is crucial just as such freedom is crucial for employees who on their own initiative may (and will) want to move about until they find their proper niche! Imperfections and injustices will always exist, but we must have the freedom in our country for the right person to fill the right spot. Ability should be the major criterion for hiring persons for jobs, not race or gender.

WOMEN IN THE MILITARY

The service academies should be for men only. While it is true that women have the intellectual ability to master the course work of West Point, and the Naval and Air Force Academies, they do not possess the physical strength to keep up with the men. A man with the limited physical powers of the females who are admitted would not be admitted.

Furthermore, the presence of women is a powerful distraction for the men. Make no mistake, their thoughts will be on sex and romance when they should be thinking about their difficult work and future careers. Even more serious is the diluting effect women have on the "male atmosphere" that once characterized life in the service academies. This "atmosphere" is very important. Part of the purpose of the four years at the academies is to develop as fully as possible aggressive, yet controlled, highly motivated leadership, and other male qualities. These men become the military elite. Any armed force must have its elite; they become the leaders. There are other sources too, but the service academies are the primary source. Women mixed with the men dilute these qualities because the leaders in the academies cannot uphold these values as forthrightly when they know there are students there (the females) who cannot achieve these goals.

Women officers are not as versatile as the men. Purely on the basis of cost-effectiveness, the taxpayer is not getting his money's worth from the women.

The solution is to admit the limited usefulness of

women in the military. War is a man's world; let us face that fact squarely and use women in those roles which history shows they can superbly fill. The services do need a female officer corps. A separate academy for training women officers would be the solution.

Except for certain courses and limited activities, women should be trained separately in the ROTC program. Follow the example of the United States Marines; they have not lost their way. They train women separately except to a very minor degree. Male recruits need male sergeants to train them. Men going into combat need men to lead them. Women can provide support and care for the wounded.

WOMEN IN THE WORK FORCE

Economic pressures as well as a variety of other factors have caused millions of women to enter the work force. This trend will undoubtedly continue for a while. There is an underlying assumption about the sexes, which is influencing the placement of women in the work force that is doing great damage to men and to women and to society in general. It is assumed that the sexes are interchangeable, that no discriminations should be made on the basis of sex. This of course is a false assumption. There are enormous differences between male and female. A corollary to this assumption, but one which is not talked about as widely, is that the sexes will react to each other in the same way. This too is false.

Women will be working and the sexes will be mixed in the work place, but to treat the sexes as equivalent in all respects and to deny the powerful forces which male and female evoke in each other is a denial of reality.

Men and women differ both physically and psychologically. It is absurdity in the extreme to force work quotas for women in heavy industry, for instance. While there may be an occasional female who is physically powerful enough to perform certain tasks, placing a woman in close proximity to men is disrupting and distracting to the men and to the woman, if she possesses the normal female instincts. Managers responsible for hiring, I believe, should have the freedom to hire those individuals who are best suited to perform the particular task *and* whose presence will not diminish the efficiency of others by virtue of the arousal of powerful biological forces, e.g., the sexual drive and its associated instincts, such as protectiveness in the male toward the female. If a female can perform a task well, and if she is sufficiently isolated from the men, or if the men are sufficiently mature and self-controlled so they can keep their minds on their work, then the female can be hired. Conversely, placing a few males in the context of an all-female work force will be just as disruptive. Managers need the freedom to decide when the sex is having a disruptive effect on the work force. If it is not, fine.

Mixing women into the intimate living quarters and intense working relationships which exist among the police and among firemen is absurd—especially so if she brings her nursing baby to work. Having her sleep in the area with the men is unfair to them all and to the wives and families of the men. Sooner or later an "affair" will develop to the great cost to all.

HOMOSEXUALITY

My best advice to parents is to watch for signs of effiminacy or evidence of homosexual inclinations or overt homosexuality in their boy children and face the problem head on. Similarly, such behavior in girls along with excessive masculinized tendencies or very infantile sexless qualities are cause for concern. If your child expresses feelings of homosexuality, or tells you that they are involved in homosexual behavior, you should take positive steps to correct his condition.

Do not condemn your child. The time for great understanding and acceptance has arrived. On the strength of this bond, the parent should take a stand against the homosexuality. Seek good professional assistance. Such help is hard to find, and unfortunately, the number of competent professionals is woefully inadequate to meet the need. However, parents should try hard to help the child find help. If the father, mother and child (regardless of age) will talk with each other, the possibility is created for the child to overcome the problem. The outcome of such an effort depends on how well established the homosexuality has become, and on factors within the family itself. By this I am referring to the degree of maturity of the parents, the depth of their relationship, and the depth and the quality of the relationships between parent and child. To expect some families to help one of their offspring overcome his homosexuality is like trying to pull himself up by his bootstraps. Other families are healthier.

Our national public health policy should include a posture on homosexuality along with other illnesses which have vast social implications. Such a public policy would stimulate the creation of both private and public treatment centers. To weave homosexuality into the fabric of society by "normalizing" the condition is destructive to both the individual and society.

Homosexuals would find themselves much less ostracized if they stopped trying to sell their condition and way of life to the general public. People do have common sense and their hostility is evoked by the gay lobby.

THE WOMEN'S LIBERATION MOVEMENT

Inequity is a fact of life and the feminist movement has corrected some which have been borne by women. Yet other inequities remain. But all of us suffer inequities; women are by no means the target for the injustices of life. Men and boys have suffered heavily through mankind's history, and will continue to bear the burden of injustice. So the feminist movement is not all bad by any means. It is not my intent to contrast the good and bad aspects of the movement. I simply wish to sound a loud and clear warning, for unless it is heeded, and if present trends continue, society will be in ever deeper trouble.

Now what is that trouble insofar as the feminist movement is concerned? First, it must be recognized that children need mothers; the best mother is the biologic mother who is mature enough to be a good mother. To break the child's bond to his/her mother before the separation-individuation process is complete (usually accomplished during the first three years of life) is a severe trauma to the developing child. Feminists tend to ignore or downplay or simply deny this well-established fact. As a consequence young mothers are being told to leave their infants and children, go to work, and that by doing so they will find their "personhood" and will also be doing their children a service; they will be learning to get along without their mothers, learn self-sufficiency and socialization. Such advice is wrong. Of course children need to leave their mothers, etc.,—but only when they are ready to do so. Mothering the young is one of the—perhaps the most—important of all human experiences. Fathering comes later.

Secondly, the feminist movement has attempted to brain-wash women into believing they can replace men in virtually all positions in the work place. This is nonsense. Women can do many tasks men do, and in some instances, they may even perform them better than most men. There are, however, many places women do not belong. Women should not be placed among men for long periods or too intimately. To do so breaks up the bonding which exists among men who are serving a common purpose and often leads to male-female pairing, which may break up a family.

Stated most simply, there is a powerful aspect of the feminist movement which is destructive to family life and to the society directly by placing women in roles and positions from which they should be excluded. To be discriminating is not discriminatory in the negative sense.

Finally, feminism supports the trend toward unisexism and role reversal. It is good the sexes are different. The key is to find the best way to utilize those differences for the best possible yield for both the individual and for society. The incredible success homosexuals are having in changing the law is another example. The gays are influencing educators and professional organizations, and have made big strides forward in their effort to convince the public that their way of life and their personal condition is normal. Now they are trying to get the laws changed so they can "marry," adopt children, and bring their influence to bear on virtually all walks of life.

Before you vote anyone into office, look into their personal lives and *look at their personality*. What a man or woman *is* determines to a large extent what he *believes*. I look very closely at the personalities and backgrounds of people who find their way into public office. Professional ethics prevents me from revealing what is glaringly obvious to me about some of our leaders who are in key positions of leadership and about some who are seeking office. You have to have a very healthy personality and a very strong will to be able to live by our best values, and when in office uphold them and stand up to other national leaders, and say "You will not cross this line." Far too many of our leaders and lawmakers lack this strength.

I do not believe our situation is hopeless, but it is one nonetheless which requires *everyone* to wake up and take stock. Put your life in the most constructive direction possible. Save your family, be the best parent you can possibly be, and then start looking after your country. America needs all of us like she has never needed our help before. If she does not receive this help soon, our way of life, and indeed our nation will almost surely cease to exist within a generation or two—or sooner. The future is in *our* hands and my message to you is a call to arms!

Footnotes

1. Sylvia Brodie, M.D. has written an excellent review article on this subject. See reference #7. The works to which she refers, which I believe are especially important, are those of Mahler, Jacobson, Spitz, Bobly, and Winnicott.
2. Ibid.
3. Thousands of articles exist which describe the impact of family patterns on the developing child. A representative article is reference #22. See also my own book, reference #62.
4. The companion piece to this book entitled *The Castrated Family,* covers childhood development in considerable detail. Theodore Lidz has written extensively on this subject. See reference #27.
5. Several articles which discuss the family patterns and personalities of drug users are reference numbers 9, 10, 17, 22, 43, 46, 47, 59, 64, 66.
6. Ibid.
7. Ibid.
8. The O'Neils (reference #39) made many sweeping assumptions about the human condition and the kinds of behavior which lead

to the happiest and most fulfilling marriage. They presented these assumptions as established fact, and many people blindly followed their advice.
9. See reference #63 (The Castrated Family).
10. See reference #63 (The Castrated Family).
11. For a review of some of the psychological and physiological differences between male and female, see references #13 and 29.
12. Recognizing its mistake, the Army has recently abandoned the co-educational training of recruits.
13. For an account of the profound differences between male-male bonding and male-female bonding, see reference #42.
14. For a discussion of this subject, see reference numbers 28 and 56.
15. I believe this is so because a rise in the prevalence of homosexuality is a function of disturbed family life. When societies break up, so too have the families. The most classic example is that of ancient Rome. See reference #21.
16. The American Psychiatric Association and the American Psychological Association no longer designate homosexuality as a mental disturbance. The Psychiatric Diagnostic Manual states homosexuality shall be classed as a psychiatric disturbance only if the individual is bothered by his/her condition. Such reasoning is a laughable, but tragic absurdity. There are many forms of mental

disturbance that do not bother the patient; in fact, the patient finds pleasure from his illness! Dr. Charles Socorides has written an article entitled The Sexual Unreason, reprinted from Book Forum: in Psychotherapy and Social Structure, Vol. I, No. 2, 1974, Hudson River Press, N.Y. which tells the sad story of how this hoax came about. In short, gay lobbying pressure, and sleight-of-hand proved to be highly effective.
17. Ibid.
18. See reference #19. In this article the author reports that the family patterns of homosexuals who were not classed as psychiatric patients are the same as those who are. Homosexuals in their claim that nothing is wrong with them point to the fact that most studies of homosexuals were done on psychiatric patients who were also homosexual.
19. See reference #4. Bieber's work is a classic. His findings are entirely consistent with the in-depth data psychoanalysts have reported.
20. Two authors stand out in my mind. Dr. Charles Socorides, references #51, 52, 53, has contributed most from a base of in-depth study and treatment of homosexuals. Dr. Frank du Maas, reference #13, discusses homosexuality from several vantage points.
21. See references #7 and 30. Natalie Shainess, M.D., an eminent psychoanalyst, has argued the point at an open debate at the American Psychiatric Association meeting and has

testified at congressional hearings on the harmful effects of pornography. Other publications on the harmful effects of pornography and its psychopathological roots are references #5, 8, 12, 23, 65.
22. See references #9, 10, 17, 46, 47, 59, 64, 66.
23. See reference #59.
24. See reference #18. For more information on the behavioral and other effects caused by prolonged marijuana use, refer to references #20, 31, 32, 35, 36, 37, 38, 41, 45.
25. Ibid.
26. See reference #63.
27. See references #25, 26, 33, 34, 48, 54, 61.

Selected Readings and Bibliography

1. Anshen, R. N., ed. *The Family: Its Function and Destiny.* Vol. 5. (Rev. ed.) New York: Harper, 1959.
2. Bartell, Gilbert D. *Group Sex: A Scientist's Eyewitness Report on the American Way of Swinging.* New York: P. H. Wyden, 1971.
3. Bauman, J., "Effects of Chronic Marijuana Use on Endocrine Function of Human Females" Read before: Marijuana, Biological Effects and Social Implications. New York, June 28-29, 1979.
4. Bieber, I. *Homosexuality—A Psychoanalytic Study.* New York: Basic Books, 1962.
5. Boulding, Elise. Women and Social Violence. *Internat. Soc. Science J.* 30 (4): 801-815, 1978.
6. Blum, R. H., et al. *Horatio Alger's Children: The Role of the Family in the Origin and Prevention of Drug Risk.* San Francisco: Jossey-Bass, 1972.
7. Brody, Sylvia. Psychoanalytic Theories of Infant Development and its Disturbances: A Critical Evaluation. *The Psychoanalytic Quarterly* 51 (4): 526-598, 1982.
8. Brownmiller, Susan. *Against Our Will: Men, Women and Rape*; also communication, Confer-

ence on Pornography and Male Sexuality, Dec. 2, 1981.
9. Chein. Narcotics Use Among Juveniles. In *Readings in Juvenile Delinquency*, T. Cavan, pp. 237-252. New York: Lippincott, 1964.
10. Chein, et al. The Family of the Addict. In *The Road to H: Narcotics, Delinquency and Social Policy.* I. Chein, pp. 251-275. New York: Basic Books, 1964.
11. Chlor, Harry M. Definitions of Obscenity and the Nature of the Obscene, *Obscenity and Public Morality.* Chicago: University of Chicago Press, 1969.
12. Donnerstein, Edward. Pornography and Violence Against Women: Experimental Studies. *Annals of New York Academy of Sciences* 347:277-288, 1980.
13. Du Maas, Frank M. *Gay Is Not Good.* Nashville: Thomas Nelson, 1979.
14. Gittelson, Natalie. *"Dominus, A Woman Looks at Men's Lives."* New York: Farrar, Straus and Giraux, 1978.
15. Goldberg, S. *The Inevitability of Patriarchy.* New York: Morrow, 1973.
16. Hart, R. H. *Better Grass—The Cruel Truth About Marijuana.* P. O. Box 7542, Shawnee Mission, Kansas: Psychoneurologia Press, 1980.
17. Hartman. Drug-Taking Adolescents. *Psychoanalytic Study of the Child* 24: 384, 1969.
18. Heath, R. G. *Marijuana and the Brain.* American Council on Marijuana, 6193 Executive Boulevard, Rockville, Maryland, 20852.
19. Hendin, Herbert. Homosexuality: The Psycho-

social Dimension. *Journal of the American Academy of Psychoanalysis* 6 (1): 479-496, 1978.
20. Jones, H. B., *What the Practicing Physician Should Know About Marijuana.* Private Practice, January, 1980.
21. Kardiner, A. *The Individual and His Society.* New York: Columbia University Press, 1939.
22. Kellman, S. G., Ensminger, M., Turner, J. Family Structure and the Mental Health of Children. *Archives of General Psychiatry,* 34: 1012-1022, September, 1977.
23. Kline, Victor B. *Where Do You Draw the Line? An Exploration into Media Violence, Pornography and Censorship.* Brigham Young University, Press, 1974.
24. Kolodny, R. C., et al. Depression of Plasma Testosterone and Acute Marijuana Administration in *The Pharmocology of Marijuana,* pp. 217-225. Raven Press, 1976.
25. Lasch, Christopher. *Haven in a Heartless World: The Family Besieged.* New York: Basic Books, 1977.
26. Lasch, Christopher. *The Culture of Narcissism: American Life in an Age of Diminishing Expectations.* 1st ed. New York: Norton, 1978, c 1979.
27. Lidz, Theodore. *The Family and Human Adaptation.* New York: International Universities Press, 1963.
28. Lidz, Theodore. The Family: The Source of Human Resources. in *Human Resources and Economic Welfare* by Ivor Berg. New York/London: Columbia University Press, 1972.
29. Maccoby, E. E., ed. *The Development of Sex Differ-*

ences. Stanford: Stanford University Press, 1966.
30. Malamuth, Neal M., Heim, M., Feshbach, S. Sexual Responsiveness of College Students to Rape Depictions: Inhibitory and Disinhibitory Effects *Journal of Personal and Social Psychology* 38 (3): 399-408.
31. Mann, Peggy. Marijuana Alert III: The Devastation of Personality. *Reader's Digest,* December 1981.
32. Marijuana, Its Health Hazards and Therapeutic Potentials, Council on Scientific Affairs, *Journal of the American Medical Association* 26 (16) October 16, 1981.
33. Millar, Thomas P. The Age of Passion Man. *Canadian Journal of Psychiatry.* 27: 679-682, 1982.
34. Montague, M. F. A., ed. *Culture and the Evolution of Man.* New York: Oxford University Press, 1962.
35. Nahas, G. G. Current Status of Marijuana Research, *Journal of the American Medical Association,* 242:2775, December 21, 1979.
36. _____. *Keep Off the Grass.* New York: Pergamon Press, 1979.
37. _____. *Marijuana—Deceptive Weed.* New York: Raven Press, 1972.
38. Nahas, G. G., Paton, W. D. M. *Marijuana: Biological Effects (Analysis, Metabolism, Cellular Responses, Reproduction, and Brain).* New York: Pergamon Press, 1979.
39. O'Neil, Neva, O'Neil, George. *Open Marriage, a New Life Style for Couples.* New York: Evans and Company, 1972.

40. Popenoe, Paul. "Fraudulent New 'Morality'". *Medical Aspects of Human Sexuality* 7 (4): 159-167, April, 1973.
41. Powelson, H. *Our Most Dangerous Drug.* Washington: Narcotics Education, Inc., 6830 Laurel St., NW, Washington, D. C., 20012.
42. Riencourt, Omairy de. *Sex and Power in History.* New York: Dell Publishing Company, 1974.
43. Rosenberg, C. M. Young Drug Addicts: Background and Personality. *Journal of Nervous and Mental Disease* 148:65, 1969.
44. Rosenkrantz, H., Fleishman, R. W. Effect of Cannabis on the Lung, *Marijuana: Biological Effects* (G. G. Nahas and W. D. M. Paton, eds.), pp. 279-299. New York: Pergamon Press, 1979.
45. Russell, George K. *Marijuana Today: A Compilation of Medical Findings for the Layman.* American Council on Marijuana, 6193 Executive Boulevard, Rockville, Maryland, 20852.
46. Savitt, R. A. Psychoanalytic Studies on Addiction: Ego Structure in Narcotic Addiction. *Psychoanalytic Quarterly* 32 (43), 1963.
47. Seldin, N. E. The Family of the Addict: A Review of the Literature. *International Journal of the Addictions,* 7 (97), 1972.
48. Sexton, P. *The Feminized Male: Classrooms, White Collar and the Decline of Manliness.* New York: Random House, 1969.
49. Smith, C. C., et al. Effect of Δ^9-Tetrahydrocannabinol (THC) on Female Reproductive Function, *Marijuana: Biological Effects* (G. G. Nahas and W. D. M. Paton, eds.), pp. 449-

467. New York: Pergamon Press, 1979.
50. Smith, Malcolm E. *"With Love from Dad."* Book Distributors, Inc., 1978.
51. Socarides, C. W. *The Overt Homosexual.* New York: Grune & Stratton, 1968.
52. _____. *Beyond Sexual Freedom.* New York: Quadrangle, 1975.
53. _____. *Homosexuality.* New York: Jason Aronson, 1978.
54. Sorokin, P. *The American Sex Revolution.* Boston: Sargent Publishers, 1956.
55. Sorokin, P. *Social and Cultural Dynamics.* New York: American Book Co., 1937.
56. Stoller, R. J. *Sex and Gender: The Development of Masculinity and Feminity.* New York: Science House, 1968.
57. Stoller, R. J. Pornography and Perversion. *Perversion: the erotic form of hatred,* pp. 63-92. New York: Pantheon Books (Random House), 1975.
58. Tashkin, D. P., Shapiro, B. J., Lee, Y. E. Subacute Effects of Heavy Marijuana Smoking on Pulmonary Function in Healthy Men. *New England Journal of Medicine* 294: 125-29, 1976.
59. Tec, N. Family and Differential Involvement with Marijuana: A Study of Suburban Teenagers. *Journal of Marriage and the Family* 32:656, 1970.
60. Turner, C., Waller, C. W., et al. *Marijuana, An Annotated Bibliography.* New York: MacMillan Information, Inc., 1976.
61. Unwin, J. D. *Sex and Culture.* London: Oxford University Press, 1934.

62. Voth, H., Orth, M. *Psychotherapy and the Role of the Environment.* New York: Behavioral Publications, 1977.
63. Voth, H. *How To Get Your Child Off Marijuana.* Darien, Conn. Patient Care Publications, 1980.
   Voth, H. The Castrated Family (Retitled).
64. Walk, R. L., Diskind, M. H. Personality Dynamics of Mothers and Wives of Drug Addicts. *Crime and Delinquency* 7: 148, 1961.
65. Wertham, Fredric. Is Exposure to Pornography Harmful to Teen-agers? *Journal of the American Medical Association* 231 (13): 1293, 1975.
66. Wiener, H., Kaplan, E. H. Drug Use in Adolescents, Psychodynamic Meaning and Pharmacologic Effect. *Psychoanalytic Study of the Child* 24: 399, 1969.